CW01022060

SKYWARD GAZE
The year UFOs captured the world

1947's legacy in pop culture

SKYWARD GAZE

The year UFOs captured the world

1947's legacy in pop culture

A quick preliminary essay

Maurizio Verga

Copyright 2023 Maurizio Verga

All rights reserved. No part of this work may be used in any form or for any purpose without prior written permission from the copyright holders. An exception is made for short extracts used for reviews of the work.

ISBN: 9798869984791

First edition (December 2023).

How to contact the author: mauverga@ufo.it

Table of contents

Chapter Summaries

1947: Saucer headlines on the front pages of newspapers **21**

The chapter analyzes the extensive newspaper coverage given to sightings of unidentified flying objects in the summer of 1947, especially between June 26 and July 8. In those days, many newspapers published front-page articles about the Kenneth Arnold's sighting and subsequent witness reports, often with large headlines. The chapter highlights how press attention was amplified by contextual factors like post-war technological developments, the Cold War, and the presence of a potentially credible witness in Arnold. Headlines emphasized the spread of sightings and military efforts to investigate them. According to the chapter, press coverage had a snowball effect, spurring more witnesses to come forward and generating a peak of interest between July 7-8. Subsequently, attention quickly faded, but the idea of flying saucers remained firmly lodged in popular imagination. The large headlines had a significant visual and emotional impact, showing the "media weight" the phenomenon had gained. They helped generate further interest and sightings in a reciprocal cause-effect cycle.

1947: How I sell you the saucer. Flying saucers soar in advertising **33**

The chapter analyzes how, in the summer of 1947, coinciding with the wave of UFO sightings in the United States, the image of "flying saucers" was immediately exploited in local newspaper advertisements. A distinction is made between actual ads using flying saucers and publicity stunts involving dropping flyers or paper plates from planes, often mistaken for sightings. The ads mainly promoted homes, cars, food, and clothing sales. They appeared predominantly between July 7-16, peaking on July 10-11. They capitalized on the phenomenon's appeal to grab attention with playful references to Martians. The paper plate drops generated many false sighting reports, but some consciously used them to promote business activities, later notifying newspapers. This represented a temporary, episodic use of the saucer image, reflecting its rapid penetration into the popular imagination. Advertisements were more frequent in the US, with rare appearances abroad.

Making the saucers popular: cartoons and comics in the 1947 press **55**

The chapter analyzes the role of cartoons and comics in spreading the image of flying saucers during the 1947 UFO wave in the United States. Satirical newspaper cartoons, especially between July 7-16, poked fun at saucers by linking them to inflation, taxes, and war anxieties. They helped create a basic saucer iconography of round objects. French satirical magazines mocked the American mania. Comic strips, very popular then, only introduced saucers after the peak of sightings, initially with ironic quips. Later, the Buck Rogers character depicted actual flying saucers, anticipating classic forms. According to the author, cartoons and comics familiarized the saucer image to the general public, profoundly shaping pop culture. From satirical sketches to realistic prototypes, they contributed to molding the visual representation.

1947: the Boyle abduction and other encounter stories 79

The chapter describes some alleged UFO sightings and close encounters with saucer pilots reported in the 1947 American press during the first significant wave of observations. It mentions the satirical story of journalist Hal Boyle, who claimed to be abducted by a Martian aboard a flying saucer. The chapter introduces the concept that, even at that time, saucers could come from Mars. Brief accounts of encounters with alleged saucer "pilots" or "little men" published in local papers are then cited. These stories seem to be mostly pranks or fictions created by journalists to capitalize on the sightings wave. The pilots were described as "little men" or exotic creatures in a parody spirit. Other journalists made fake interviews with Martians who arrived in saucers as a rhetorical device to comment on the political and social situation. The chapter analyzes how many elements of these counterfeit stories anticipate the more classic abduction and contactee narratives of the 1950s: pilot morphology, vehicle technical features, and Martian origin. These were parodies and jokes aimed at discrediting the saucer phenomenon, which was receiving massive media attention. Some narrative ideas would later be recovered and reinterpreted more "seriously" by other witnesses.

Here they are! Early crashes of flying saucers: a short visual history 99

This chapter describes various cases of fake "flying saucers" found on the ground or purposefully created during the 1947 UFO wave in the United States (including several local balloon crashes that didn't get the massive nationwide hype of the Roswell story). These were primarily pranks or publicity stunts. It illustrates several incidents where makeshift discs, clearly made from scrap materials and technological parts, were found. They often ended up on local newspapers' front pages. In some cases, the Army or FBI was called in to investigate. Other times, organized launches of fake paper discs were done from planes for promotional purposes. Hundreds or thousands of these gadgets were dropped on cities to advertise festivals, referendums, and military recruitment, to name a few. The chapter visually documents these episodes with captions from period newspapers, providing an amusing and colorful fresco of how the sightings wave was exploited through various gimmicks.

Day one of the saucer era in the press 128

The chapter discusses the newspaper coverage on June 26, 1947, of Kenneth Arnold's sighting of "flying saucers" in the skies over Washington state. This event is considered the starting point of the modern UFO phenomenon. The author analyzes over 300 articles published that day, examining aspects like headlines, front page placement, and content. It highlights the crucial role of the *Associated Press* in rapidly spreading Arnold's story nationwide. About 42% of articles appeared on the front pages, indicating the event's perceived importance. Headlines often emphasized the objects' estimated speed (1,200 mph) and Arnold's credibility as a pilot. Sensationalist terms like "disc" and (more rarely) Mars references helped capture the reader's attention. The author observes how press coverage lent legitimacy to Arnold's account and triggered an avalanche of further witness reports in the following days. The press helped cement the idea of those mysterious contraptions as "flying saucers" in the public imagination, although Arnold's original description referred to crescent-shaped objects. The article provides detailed statistics and in-depth analysis based on a large sample of period newspapers.

Introduction

1947 was the year when the flying saucers began to appear in the skies of the United States. Isnt'it?

The answer is yes from the point of view of social history and popular culture. Still, it could be "maybe" when considering the presence of anomalous aerial sightings in the preceding decades and the widespread idea of aliens (Martians) being able to communicate with us or even visit our planet.

Anyway, 1947 was a fundamental point of distinction for modern pop culture, and the flying saucers quickly became a significant part of it. Beginning June 26, the term "flying saucer" (although already used for decades in trap shooting, as outlined by Chris Aubeck[1]) was exposed to a vast majority of the US public, and shortly afterward also abroad, associated with the idea of something technologically weird. In hours, the saucers produced tremendous hype, generating awe and possibly some sort of fear and alarm. Then it faded away a week or so, and then it rose again, even more robust and with overwhelming power, becoming nearly immediately a widespread veritable cultural phenomenon. Fueled by the press (and the increasingly important radio alike), the saucers became the national hot topic throughout a summer week. It was one of the very cases when a brand new topic was encapsulated into the popular culture and the people's imagination in a matter of days. A 1947 poll reported that over 90% of Americans had heard about flying saucers.

In an earlier book[2], I discussed the birth of the flying saucers (later evolving into UFOs and then in the modern "UFO phenomenon") in that year, focusing on the presence of the idea, both serious and ironic, that those mysterious gadgets could be from Mars. This book is a brief anthology of some articles published in the second half of the 2010s in a small UFO e-zine named "Cielo Insolito." Unlike the book, those articles covered a few specific social aspects of the massive 1947 wave of flying saucer sightings and the hype it produced.

---

1 Chris Aubeck (2023), "Saucers" - independently published.

2 Maurizio Verga (2020), "Flying saucers in the sky" - independently published.

For example, many US newspapers published large headlines on their front pages, giving top exposure to the saucer news and contributing to making them known to a vast public. The dailies had different approaches to the topic, ranging from ignoring it - or nearly - to publishing more articles in the same edition. The flying saucers became so popular, inspiring a feeling of technological breakthrough, to be immediately exploited in local advertising too. Those flying contraptions were extraordinary to make anything associated with them outstanding, including a wide variety of products, assets, or services.

Designers quickly assimilated saucers into their cartoons published in the newspapers (sometimes even on their front pages). They were a new, catchy, and ironic way to depict some issues or situations of the time, helping the saucers to become increasingly popular. But their popularity grew even more when they were included in the sought-after newspaper comics. A pretty long series of Buck Rogers strips published in late 1947 show a quick evolution in the shapes of the depicted saucers, finally showing the best prototype of the later saucer imagery, including an extraordinary disc-shaped spaceship with a dome, antenna, portholes, and beam rays.

Many newspapers published reports about crude and funny gadgets found in the courtyards of many houses and introduced as a sample of those mysterious flying saucers. The desire to joke and generate local sensation, as well as the presence of significant rewards for those bringing a "real" saucer, boosted the number of these episodes. There were also several recoveries of landed balloons. Still, none of them got the massive exposure of the seminal Roswell crash (although the stories were pretty similar) that, in the 1980s, got a significant presence in the popular culture on its own.

In 1947, you can find most but all of the elements and features of the flying saucer craze in the 1950s and the UFO phenomenon and myth in later decades. Close encounters of the third kind (when "Martians" were seen in association with the saucers) and abductions (when a person is brought aboard a "spaceship") were occasionally reported by the press.
However, they were rumors or humorous articles written by journalists. Hundreds of newspapers in the USA syndicated the hilarious two-part Hal Boyle's report of his kidnapping aboard a Martian flying saucer.

In the summer of 1947, something peculiar likely happened in the skies over the American Northwest. On June 24th, private pilot Kenneth Arnold reported seeing nine fast-moving, crescent-shaped objects while flying near Mount Rainier in Washington state. The objects zoomed by at astonishing speeds Arnold estimated at over 1,200 mph—far faster than any known aircraft at the time.

Newspapers across the country quickly picked up and sensationalized Arnold's odd account. Reporters seized on his attempt to describe the objects' movement: "like a saucer, if you skip it across the water." The next day, several hundreds of articles were published with mysterious headlines about "flying saucers." The term stuck in the public imagination even though Arnold never said he saw literal saucers.

In the following weeks, thousands more sighting reports flooded in from shocked citizens and even commercial pilots. The feverish press coverage gave rise to one of the strangest phenomena of postwar America: a UFO frenzy that's still analyzed to this day.

This book will illustrate how flying saucers left a colorful mark on mid-century America. They penetrated advertising, dominated headlines for weeks, and spooked citizens coast-to-coast—before fading mysteriously into the cultural imagination as an enduring symbol of exotic science and technology. We'll showcase press clippings and imagery to examine this fleeting, influential historical moment.

To appreciate why flying saucers captivated the nation so intensely, surveying that era's historical context and cultural landscape is necessary. Americans found themselves in an anxious new world in 1947—emerging from the terrific devastation of the Second World War while the Cold War threatened new conflicts.

Advancements in atomic weapons and rocketry sparked both optimism about technology's potential and fear of its destructive power. The press was positioned to amplify public interest—and hysteria—around flying objects spotted across the skies.

In August 1945, Americans exploded into celebration upon Japan's surrender and the victory over Germany—but the exuberance was short-lived.

The existence of a horrifying new "super weapon," the atomic bomb, soon overshadowed Japan's retreat. Its devastation of Hiroshima and Nagasaki closed the war yet introduced distressing new realities about technological warfare.

As stories and images slowly surfaced from the decimated Japanese cities in late 1945, the American public reckoned with the awesome and disturbing power unlocked by science as a whole. While some heralded atomic weapons as the ultimate insurance for peace, more profound anxieties brewed about arms races and new global threats. The nuclear bomb (and other advanced technologies) came to symbolize the postwar future—at once full of promise and peril.

Fascination with the bomb also cultivated a public appetite for speculation about clandestine military initiatives and more amazing "secret weapons" possibly in development. When odd sightings occurred in American skies just two years after the end of the Second World War, theories instantly turned to classified aircraft or weapons tests—explanations the government never confirmed. Renewed tensions with the Soviet Union fueled these theories as the Cold War began taking shape after the allies' unity collapsed.

The flying objects of 1947 must also be viewed in light of aviation's meteoric rise during the mid-20th century. The US military emerged from the war with vastly advanced aeronautic capabilities thanks hugely to the jet engine and aerodynamic innovations captured in Nazi Germany. Commercial aviation was also progressing swiftly, with passenger air travel newly available to everyday citizens. Americans were taking to the skies like never before.

US and Allied investigative teams combed all industrial and research facilities in Germany in search of advanced Luftwaffe designs for delta wings, supersonic ramjets, exotic propulsion concepts, rockets, missiles, and many other aviation-related topics.
With aviation technologies rapidly evolving and a regular flow of astounding rumors about Nazi wonder weapons (sometimes described as sci-fi Buck Rogers gadgets), the public imagination could readily conceive of mysterious aircraft exhibiting extreme speeds or unusual maneuvers. That magic German science had been looted by the Soviets, too, so the possibility that superplanes could have been built in Russia was definitely plausible.

So Kenneth Arnold's sighting of nine bat-winged objects blazing by at 1,200 mph, as fast as any bullet, did not severely challenge assumptions. Their crescent shape even resembled new swept-wing models, like the exciting Northrop flying wing. Though the reported speed stunned pilots, it was conceivable that aeronautics pushed boundaries. Most of the public had the context to accept Arnold's sighting as some radical new airplane rather than visiting spaceships. Their extraterrestrial origins evolved later as more sightings emerged with no explanations, and the ever-present idea of advanced Martians communicating with or visiting Earth became increasingly more potent. In contrast, the possibility of an American or Soviet secret weapon became less credible and lost its allure.
This book intends to chronicle a pivotal time when the flying saucer entered mainstream discourse and lodged itself into popular culture—where it remains today as a science fiction trope and focal point of conspiracy theories. Thanks to comprehensive research into newspaper archives, I'll analyze how the media's treatment of Arnold's report spiraled into a nationwide obsession.

This book intends to chronicle, quickly and in a summary fashion, a pivotal time when the flying saucer entered mainstream discourse and lodged itself into popular culture—where it remains today as a science fiction trope and focal point of conspiracy theories. Thanks to a comprehensive, 13-year-long research into newspaper archives, I'll analyze how the media's treatment of Arnold's report spiraled into a sort of nationwide obsession.

I'll quickly try to explore questions like: What about that initial sighting spawned such intensity? Why did "flying saucer" itself become such a cultural phenomenon as hats, songs, and cocktails embraced the term? How did creative hoaxes escalate public curiosity?

While the extraterrestrial nature of the sightings remains entirely inconclusive, their social impact is undeniable. This book will illustrate how flying saucers left a colorful mark on mid-century America. They penetrated advertising, dominated headlines for weeks, and spooked citizens coast-to-coast—before fading mysteriously into the cultural imagination as an enduring symbol of fabulous super science. I'll showcase press clippings and imagery to examine this fleeting, influential historical moment.

In 1947, the saucers quickly created a huge hype and technological mythology able to generate new sightings. A self-sustained process ignited a closed, nearly endless cycle still around today, although with less intensity and with significant differences.

1947: Saucer headlines on the front pages of newspapers

On the morning of Thursday, June 26, 1947, most American newspapers delivered their readers curious news from an Associated Press dispatch. A man flying in his airplane over the northwest of the country (in search of the crash site of an airplane disaster that happened months before) reported the sighting of nine "missiles" or, anyhow, odd objects flying at the stunning speed of 1,200 miles per hour.

The Oregon Statesman

FOUNDED 1651

Mystery Missiles Reported Over Cascades

Pilot Sees 'Disk-shaped Objects' Flying at 1200 Miles per Hour Above Western Washington Range

Finale of Transfer Set Today

Of Steel Mills Cut

The Oregon Statesman June 26, 1947

Those contraptions had a bizarre course: the man said it looked like that of saucers thrown on a water surface and bouncing on it. The headline writers of some newspapers liked the image of those saucers evoked by the witness. After all, those guys were always searching for concise and simple sentences to be understood immediately and powerful enough to visualize an image in readers' minds.

Bremerton Woman, 2 Midwest Men Say They Saw Disks

•LABOR LAW MUST BE ENFORCED, SAYS TRUMAN, PLEDGING HIS AID

A. F. L., C. I. O. Reject General-Strike Pleas

SHOWERS

The Seattle Daily Times

NIGHT FINAL

LATE WORLD NEWS

MAin 0300 SEATTLE, WASHINGTON, THURSDAY, JUNE 26, 1947. 3 SECTIONS, 36 PAGES PRICE FIVE CENTS

Seattle Daily Times June 26, 1947

In the title and the body of the articles, the word "saucer" began to appear to describe those things reported by more and more people in the American skies. Just because they were "flying," they were soon named "flying saucers," one of the more powerful and fascinating words of the XX century popular culture. You can find a trace of the brand-new name even in articles published on June 26.

Day after day of that summer, a strong evocative image was associated with such saucers. It was vigorously spread by the press (in the US at first, then virtually everywhere, though in different ways) and consequently more and more in-depth into the popular imagination until it consolidated and became the ultimate heritage of popular culture. The image of saucers was strong because of the combination of a shape so unusual to be inevitably the product of a super-advanced technology (therefore a mysterious one) with the action of flying, specifically a flight displaying fantastic performances.

MORE SEE FLAT, FAST DISCS CAVORTING IN SKY

San Antonio Express

LATE EDITION

MEMBER ASSOCIATED PRESS—LEASED WIRE SERVICE UNITED PRESS

VOL. LXXXII—NO. 178—82ND YEAR C SAN ANTONIO, TEXAS, FRIDAY MORNING, JUNE 27, 1947 PRICE 5 CENTS—ESTABLISHED 1865

San Antonio Express June 27, 1947

The press was the key to the disclosure of the original news, but above all, it was the key to the success of the sighting stories among most readers, who quickly fell in love or even went crazy for them. Thanks to the concomitance of some lucky circumstances, the majority of the newspapers of that time devoted a large or even massive space to the sightings, though emphasis and comments were varied. Several papers published large headlines and articles on their front pages (often more than one on the same front page). In contrast, others scattered many pieces in the same edition (mainly between July 7 and 10). They published letters from readers, pictures, and cartoons, often giving some sort of reliability to the tales of the people reporting the sightings.

Other newspapers had smaller coverage, usually just reprinting the dispatches from the wire services. Some other papers gave a tiny space to those stories, usually after July 5 or 6, when it was strictly necessary because of the emerging power of the saucers nationwide, even though they were treated as pure nonsense. Local weeklies usually had a restrictive approach, devoting little or no space to the argument: they had few pages dedicated entirely to their territory's everyday life and events. When they published something, it was just to say that something had also been seen in their area.

The predisposition (in that precise time frame) of the newswire services and, consequently, of the newspapers to devote some space to the unusual stories of citizens reporting something weird flying in the sky was also helped and boosted by other factors.

A few of them:

- An impetuous techno-scientific development, seen nearly like some sort of "magic." It made plausible the presence of flying machines with unimaginable performances.
- The Cold War with the Soviet Union. It made realistic the threat of foreign planes or "missiles," possibly developed after the amazing Nazi technologies that were regularly reported and fantasized since 1945.
- The presence of a seemingly reliable witness, a pilot who was flying, and flight was a serious business.
- The predisposition of a minority of the population in believing that there was a possible connection between the new sky intruders and the fantastic stories about Martians and their contacts published in the previous decades by the newspapers, the Sunday comics, and the sci-fi pulp magazines.

Without the combination of all those elements (and others) in an appropriate temporal and geographical frame, and without the presence of other witnesses that at midday of that Thursday, June 26 (after reading the very first news about the Arnold sighting) got in touch with some reporter to tell they too had seen something unusual, the flying saucers would have remained just a curious news appeared in the US press in the early summer of 1947.

Though the Arnold story was published just less than 24 hours later (on June 25) by the local newspaper *East Oregonian*, on June 26, it was published by hundreds of American dailies. We found more than 350 of them at this time, and over 150 newspapers published an article on their front page. The story was primarily published in other pages, usually a quarter of a column. In some cases, it covered significant placements on the front pages, rarely with titles of three or more columns. For example, *The Oregon Statesman* had a five-column article on the front page, probably the most detailed one (together with the one from the *Herald and News*) describing the Arnold episode that day.

The Northwest newspapers were those dealing more with the story of the sighting, likely because it happened just in that same area. In the following days and weeks, many of them published a significant quantity of articles (and of physical space on the paper) about the local and national sightings, comments, cartoons, advertisements, and custom news related to the flying saucers. Again, on June 26, the last edition of a Seattle newspaper had a top headline introducing the sightings of other witnesses indirectly confirming Arnold's tale, making it stronger and more believable.

The day after, a Texas newspaper (but others did the same) published a large headline, running across the front page in its last evening edition, announcing other witnesses who, after reading the news of the Arnold sighting, contacted reporters to tell what they saw.

The many articles published in the morning of June 26 were a sort of detonator triggering a "me too" phenomenon, pushing more and more people to tell their local newspapers what they had seen after (or even before) June 24. A "snowball effect" generated the peak on July 7 and 8, then melting pretty quickly. Despite this, a strong trace remained, encapsulating into the popular culture with stunning strength and speed. Why this? Likely, it was due to the proper context and to the presence of specific motifs in the imagination of the time (for example, the underground idea of the existence of Martians technologically and scientifically much more advanced than humankind) that fitted well with the mystery of the outlandish flying objects showing stunning performances.

Frontpage headlines reappeared on July 4, but above all, on July 5. The beginning of five days saw the overwhelming explosion of the wave of sightings. All parts of American society were touched by such a saucer craze thanks to massive media coverage (including the radio). Such coverage was fueled by the unexpected interest of the public in the saucers, and it interacted intensely with them, following a reciprocal cause-effect process.

LEWISTON MORNING TRIBUNE

Established September, 1892 (AP)—Associated Press LEWISTON, IDAHO, SATURDAY, JULY 5, 1947 8 Pages Single Copies Five Cents

UAL Crew Reports Nine Huge Discs Over Idaho

Lewiston Morning Tribune July 5, 1947

Between July 7 and 8, large headlines running across the whole front page were several, but even more those with showy headlines placed in lower sections of the front pages. Starting July 9, they became fewer and then extremely rare after July 10.

Large headlines delivering a great visual and emotional impact were specific to the American scene. A noteworthy exception was Brazil (and Mexico to a lesser extent), where some newspapers published even larger headlines on their front pages from July 8 until the end of that month. Saucer headlines were unthinkable for the European newspapers (including the Italian ones, which had as little as four pages due to post-war paper shortage), even in the early fifties when the phenomenon had become popular in the old continent.

Most large headlines on the front pages of 1947 could be grouped into a few topics:

- local sightings ("they arrived here too")
- the spread of sightings in more and more states ("increasingly people saw these things, so something real must be out there")
- planes patrolling the skies hunting the saucers ("we want to find them, and see them closely")
- the "saucer" recovered by the Army at Roswell ("at last the Army got one of them so that the mystery will be solved")

In most front-page headlines, terms like "disc" and "disk" were frequently used more than in titles of articles published on inside pages. Likely, it was just a simple choice of headline writers for shorter words better fitting the limited length of those titles.

These headlines' visual and emotional power (we just offered a small selection of published ones) was remarkable. They showed the "mediatic weight" gained by the saucers; the press rewarded such a "weight" with those unusual spaces, satisfying the fascinated curiosity of the readers.

Moreover, those headlines generated new interest in saucers, new awareness about the presence of strange things in the sky, and ultimately, new sightings from those who felt authorized to see what the newspapers reported, becoming a protagonist of that extraordinary popular event[3].

Then, all ended quickly, in fewer days than those previously necessary to reach the peak. But just apparently. The saucers in those headlines remained firmly docked to the imagination of most of the population, not only those who believed the stories reported by the newspapers but even those who just smiled or laughed at them.

DISCOS VOADORES SOBRE SÃO PAULO

A NOITE S. PAULO

A Noite July 12, 1947

---

3 According to some researchers, another factor helping the saucers get space in the newspapers was some deficiency of "strong" news (which would have cut down other headlines and spaces). Though I didn't do any specific in-depth analysis of the general news in those days, it seems that the American newspapers already had enough uncommon international and local news to deal with. The flying saucers earned their own celebrity.

VOLUME 40, NUMBER 4 — OXNARD, CALIFORNIA, SATURDAY, JULY 5, 1947 — PRICE FIVE CENTS

FLYING SAUCERS SAID 'DELUSION BRED BY ATOMIC WAR SCARE'

MacKenzie to Manage Dock Again

B. R. MacKenzie, who was manager of Dock No. 1 at Port Hueneme when the Navy purchased it from the Harbor District, will return to that post when the Harbor Commissioners

Mystery Discs 'Sighted' by Persons in All Areas; Army Begins Investigation

Inventor Here?

A young Oxnard man may be the inventor of the "flying saucer."

Scientists Smile

By Paul F. Ellis
United Press Science Writer

Reports of "flying saucers"

Figura 4 - Oxnard Press Courier 5 luglio 1947

DAY BY DAY
Picnic tables in Washington County and surrounding areas were at a premium yesterday.

THE Daily Mail.

WEATHER
Clear tonight. Sunday increasing cloudiness and continued warm.

VOL. CXIX, NO. 157. — HAGERSTOWN, MD., SATURDAY, JULY 5, 1947. — SINGLE COPY, 5 CENTS.

"Flying Discs" Seen In Different Areas

From Our Reporters' Notebook

Three women, each from a different state, met at the same counter in a Hagerstown store one afternoon this week. The conversation was overheard by a local housewife, who was making a purchase. The clerk had just finished

Fireworks Kill Four Of 224 Who

Town Completely Isolated By Worst Mississippi Flood In Its History

Necessities Being Supplied Illinois Community By Boat; Crest Expected Today With

Want To Learn Full Terms Of

Scores Report Seeing "Saucers" Traveling At Tremendous Speeds

Figura 5 - The Daily Mail 5 luglio 1947

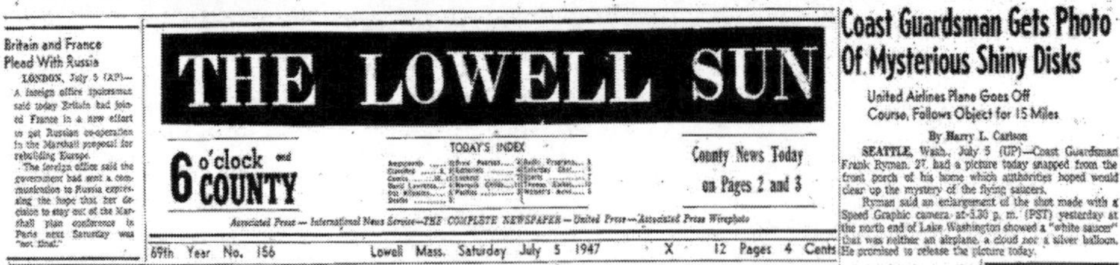

"FLYING SAUCERS" WHIZZING THROUGH NORTHWESTERN USA

Britain and France Plead With Russia

LONDON, July 5 (AP)— A foreign office spokesman said today Britain had joined France in a new effort to get Russian co-operation in the Marshall proposal for rebuilding Europe.

The foreign office said the government had sent a communication to Russia expressing the hope that her decision to stay out of the Marshall plan conference in Paris next Saturday was "not final."

THE LOWELL SUN

6 o'clock and COUNTY

TODAY'S INDEX

County News Today on Pages 2 and 3

Associated Press — International News Service—THE COMPLETE NEWSPAPER — United Press — Associated Press Wirephoto

69th Year No. 156 — Lowell Mass. Saturday July 5 1947 — X — 12 Pages 4 Cents

Coast Guardsman Gets Photo Of Mysterious Shiny Disks

United Airlines Plane Goes Off Course, Follows Object for 15 Miles

By Harry L. Carlson

SEATTLE, Wash., July 5 (UP)—Coast Guardsman Frank Ryman, 27, had a picture today snapped from the front porch of his home which authorities hoped would clear up the mystery of the flying saucers.

Ryman said an enlargement of the shot made with a Speed Graphic camera at 3:30 p. m. (PST) yesterday at the north end of Lake Washington showed a "white saucer" that was neither an airplane, a cloud nor a silver balloon. He promised to release the picture today.

Figura 6 - The Lowell Sun 5 luglio 1947

Weather
Partly cloudy, warm.

The Brownsville Herald

SUNDAY EDITION

Serving The Rio Grande Valley For Over 50 Years

56TH YEAR — NO. 2 — (P) MEMBER — BROWNSVILLE, TEXAS, SUNDAY, JULY 6, 1947 — 42 Pages — PRICE 10c

FLYING DISC MYSTERY BAFFLES AMERICA

Figura 7 - The Brownsville Herald 6 luglio 1947

THE RED STREAK

Spokane Daily Chronicle

61ST YEAR. NO. 348. 24 PAGES SPOKANE, WASH., MONDAY, JULY 7, 1947. PRICE FIVE CENTS. PHONE MAIN 1131.

DISK SEEN CLOSE-UP, IS CLAIM

Figura 8 - Spokane Daily Chronicle 7 luglio 1947

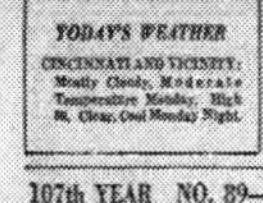

TODAY'S WEATHER
CINCINNATI AND VICINITY: Mostly Cloudy, Moderate Temperature Monday; High 86. Clear, Cool Monday Night.

THE CINCINNATI ENQUIRER

Copyright, 1947, the Cincinnati Enquirer

FINAL EDITION

107th YEAR NO. 89—DAILY 20 PAGES MONDAY MORNING, JULY 7, 1947 ***** FIVE CENTS

FLYING SAUCERS OVER CINCINNATI

Army Aircraft Search For Mystery Discs

Figura 9 - The Cincinnati Enquirer 7 luglio 1947

International News Service
International Illustrated News Picture Service

THE EVENING TRIBUNE

UNION COUNTY'S HOME DAILY

WEATHER

Vol. XXXIX, No. 239. MARYSVILLE, OHIO, MONDAY, JULY 7, 1947 By Carrier 15c a Week

'SAUCERS' AROUSE NATIONWIDE INTEREST

Figura 10 - The Marysville Evening Tribune 7 luglio 1947

The Weather

The Vidette-Messenger

Special Events

Vol. 21—No. 2 Telephones 13 and 14 Valparaiso, Indiana, Monday, July 7, 1947 The Home of Valparaiso University Five Cents

REPORTS SPOTTING 'DISC' HERE

Figura 11 - The Vidette Messenger 7 luglio 1947

THE SPOKESMAN-REVIEW

65TH YEAR. NO. 54. MONDAY MORNING. JULY 7, 1947. PRICE FIVE CENTS SPOKANE, WASH.

"SAUCER" REPORTS INCREASE AS SKY IS SEARCHED IN VAIN

$5,000,000,000 HOLE IN U.S. TAX SACK

Treasury Seeks to

ARMY SAYS DAMS WON'T HURT FISH

Only One of Several

They Say They Saw Mysterious "Flying Saucers" in Northwest

Group of Flying Disks Said to Have Hit on Mountain Near Idaho Town.

Figura 12 - The Spokesman review 7 luglio 1947

TIMES UNION
5 CENTS FINAL
NO. 12380—DAILY ALBANY, N. Y., MONDAY, JULY 7, 1947
18 PAGES—2 SECTIONS
COAST PLANES HUNT FLYING DISCS
Horses Wander Across Hudson
Seek Key to Mystery in Northwest

Figura 13 - Twin Falls Times Union 7 luglio 1947

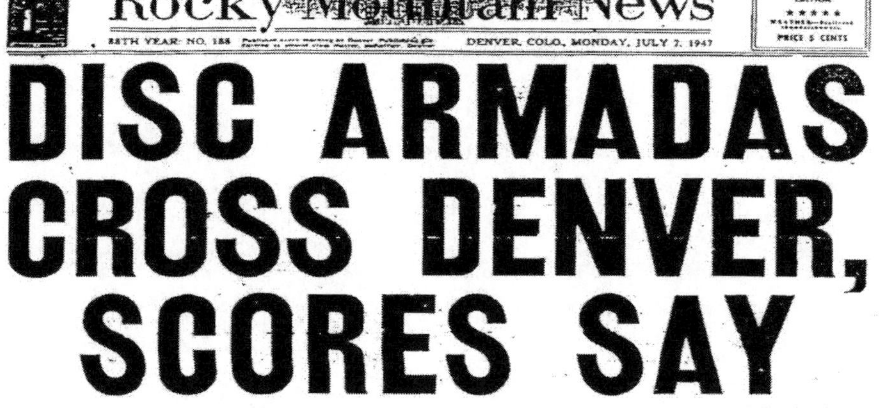
Rocky Mountain News
SUNRISE EDITION
PRICE 5 CENTS
DENVER, COLO., MONDAY, JULY 7, 1947
DISC ARMADAS CROSS DENVER, SCORES SAY
—STORY ON PAGE 5

Figura 14 - Rocky Mountain News 7 luglio 1947

FLYING DISC FOUND IN NEW MEXICO
Latest Associated Press News
Ellensburg Daily Record
The Weather
Vol. 36. Member Associated Press
ELLENSBURG, WASHINGTON TUESDAY, JULY 8, 1947
No. 170

Figura 15 - Ellensburg Daily Record 8 luglio 1947

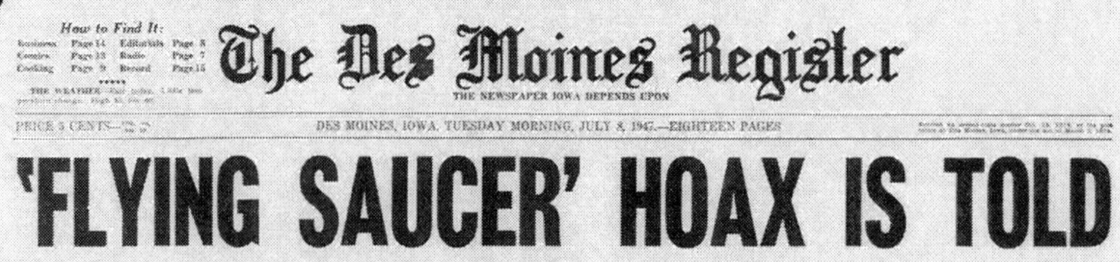
How to Find It:
The Des Moines Register
THE NEWSPAPER IOWA DEPENDS UPON
DES MOINES, IOWA, TUESDAY MORNING, JULY 8, 1947.—EIGHTEEN PAGES
'FLYING SAUCER' HOAX IS TOLD

Figura 16 - The Des Moines Register 8 luglio 1947

THE BELLINGHAM HERALD
Vol. LVII, No. 82
Bellingham, Wash., Tuesday, July 8, 1947
FINAL
'FLYING DISK' FOUND, SAYS ARMY

Figura 17 - The Bellingham Herald 8 luglio 1947

American League Beats Nationals, 2 to 1, in Tight All-Star Game

DETAILS AND WIREPHOTO, PAGE 14

DISK LANDS ON RANCH IN N. M.; IS HELD BY ARMY

Figura 18 - The Seattle Daily Times 8 luglio 1947

News Behind The News

Revolt

THE WEATHER

ARMY SAYS HAS DISC

Figura 19 San Mateo Times 8 luglio 1947

PARA AUMENTO DO EFETIVO DA POLICIA MUNICIPAL

"DISCOS VOADORES" VISTOS NO BRASIL

Passaram à grande velocidade e altura no hinterland paulista — Avistados, também, em outras partes da América Latina — Apreendido um dos misteriosos discos, caído num rancho do Novo México — A Rússia e Orson Welles nada têm a ver com a atual agitação...

Figura 20 - A Manha 9 luglio 1947

FLYING DISK PROVES TO BE FLUKE

Object Said To Be Army Weather Kite

Figura 21 - Herald and News 9 luglio 1947

1947: How I sell you the saucer. Flying saucers soar in advertising

In the last week of June 1947, thanks to a series of particular combinations that emerged in the United States of America, the stories of the observations of "flying saucers" were born and developed prodigiously. Their image and the emotional evocation they produced entered the collective imagination and the popular culture of the time with incredible speed. These elements were so strong and penetrated the collective imagination that they were immediately considered to be a new and suitable subject to convey advertising messages at the local level, primarily through the press.

The advertising inserts, which ranged from the simple economic announcement to the entire page (but only occasionally), could be summarized into some main macro-groups:

- Economic announcements for the sale of houses or cars
- Promotion of restaurants or food
- Promotion of clothing
- Promotion of other products or events, including simple references to disks within "normal" advertisements
- Text announcements (limited titles, no images or drawings, essentially simple advertising texts)

It is also necessary to consider a particularly significant "phenomenon" from a quantitative point of view: the launch from advertising airplanes of leaflets or real paper plates. In both cases, numerous "sightings" of disks were generated, which were easily identifiable and often explained as such even at the time. Still, the paper plates sometimes conveyed advertising messages directly linked to the idea of the flying saucer.

The great majority of paper advertisements appeared in local daily newspapers for ads of equally local activities. Although some of them were repeated for two or more days, the intensive advertising exploitation of the subject of disks lasted a little less than ten days. Then, the announcements became episodic and mainly aimed at seizing the enormous clamor that the topic had aroused among the population, placing itself in its wake and exhausting itself as it diminished.

Trenton Evening Times May 9, 1947

From a quantitative point of view, all those advertisements represented only a tiny fraction of the clippings published by American newspapers in that period.

BEFORE ARNOLD

In the months before Arnold's June 24 observation, some advertisements based on the popular image of the Martian appeared in American newspapers, which seemed to have some relevance to the advertising messages that materialized during the summer to exploit the considerable impact of the flying disk phenomenon. It is worth noting that a limited number of inserts are available, and above all because the research conducted so far has focused on terms like "disks" or "Martians," and only thanks to some alternative keywords to the latter term have we come across them.

The Times 25 gennaio 1947

On January 25, a local American newspaper published the announcement of a conference (integrated with a seven-and-a-half-minute color film) entitled "Signs from another world," held by a local Seventh-day Adventist church exponent. It seems that topics such as atomic energy, the sending of radar signals to the Moon (an experiment that had just been carried out by the US Army and which was popularly perceived as another staggering technological milestone), astronomical phenomena, and meteor showers had a meaning (the "signs from another world" of the title).

The rhetorical figure of the Martian, seen as an extraordinary being endowed with superior knowledge (a concept still present in the current modern popular culture), was still quite frequent at that time, as it had been in previous decades.

Even the Man From Mars
Can See This Bargain
3-Room brick, living room with fireplace, dining room, kitchen with plenty of cabinets, tiled drain, 2 large bedrooms, 1 bedroom 14x18, floor furnace. Stairs to attic storage, Textoned, tiled bath, shower. On Amherst handy to Inwood shopping center. Would GI with $800. Total price $10,800. Mr. Alger, L-2106.
C. C. McLAIN
4017 Cedar Springs.

Dalllas Morning News February 8, 1947

Advertising made frequent use of it. In February, for example, a Texan newspaper chose it to advertise a real estate sale: "Even the Martian can realize this deal." Another inhabitant of Mars, depicted in a bizarre way but with the usual macrocephalic appearance, was used to promote a germicide for preserving furs and woolen garments. The large ad, a quarter page, was published several times during May, for example, in the *Trenton Evening Times*.

FLYING SAUCERS TO SELL

Wilmington News Journal July 7, 1947

At the moment, it seems that the first advertisement incorporating flying disks into its message appeared on July 7, the same day the American press published the most significant number of articles on the new phenomenon. An insurance agency, or whoever was responsible for it, had probably perceived, likely a few days earlier, that those strange things in the sky that everyone was talking about could be an excellent way to draw attention to their own business.

The next day, there was a sort of explosion in advertisements using the term "flying saucers" or "flying discs." The peak was reached between July 10 and 11 (when the news of the sightings and comments on the whole affair were already waning), but the inserts remained quite numerous until mid-July. As expected, there was a temporal lag of a few days between the peak of journalistic coverage of the sightings and the intensive exploitation of their evocation through advertising messages.

-Lewiston Morning Tribune July 9, 1947

The Victoria Advocate July 8, 1947

Those investing in advertising decided to use the disks as part of their promotion after realizing the staggering space they had gained in American newspapers and, therefore, in the minds of tens of millions of readers. Radio at that time also dedicated news and some "specials" to the topic. Still, it is impossible to know if radio advertising messages also referred to the topic.

On July 8, a California newspaper published a nice illustrated ad promoting a local car dealership. It depicted a disk (similar to an artistic reconstruction of the disks that had appeared in the press a few days earlier) equipped with what seemed to be a sort of rear jet engine. Even the bizarre pilot was utterly human, sitting in front of a steering wheel and with a cup of coffee over his head (a clear, humorous note associated with the presence of the disk, i.e., the "saucer"). He wanted to exchange his flying disk for a 1946 or 1947 car model, and others were coming up behind him. In the text below, the pilot was quoted continuing his chatter, at one point referring to the inhabitants of his planet as "Saturnian morons."

Long Beach Independent July 8, 1947

The ad in a Texas newspaper on July 8 was particularly witty: it invited people to observe the flying disks from their own backyard, comfortably seated on promotional garden chairs and armchairs.

On July 9th, more and more newspapers published advertisements on the subject. In one, it was announced that the disks could be missiles coming from Mars, but only tires were sold by a local business.

In another, the semantic commonality between the disc-shaped objects flying in the sky (less frequently indicated as "discs" or "disks") and those spinning on gramophones was used to promote the musical record of two singers (unknown print source). A full hundred dollars of the time were promised in the advertisement of a camera seller to whoever presented the "best" photograph of a flying saucer.

Between July 10th and 16th, the number of advertisements increased further, and some of them were of particular interest and demonstrated specific creativity in making the best use of the evocation of this new and effervescent mass phenomenon.

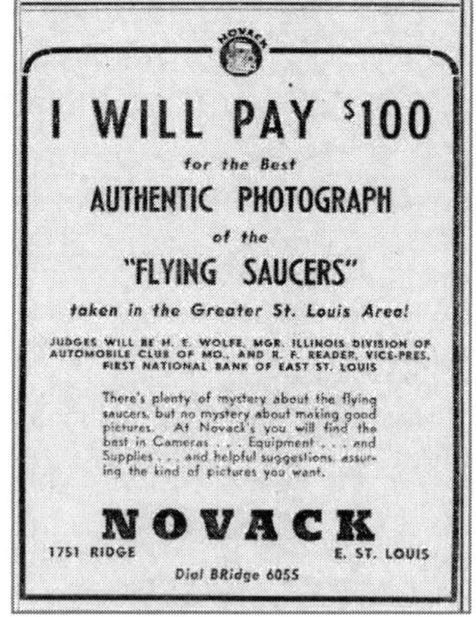

St. Louis Post Dispatch July 9, 1947

However, with the passing days, the titles inevitably became smaller or even tended to disappear over the weeks. The disks had penetrated the popular imagination and sedimented there strongly, but market rules had to be applied. The furor over the topic had abated; people talked about it less frequently, so the disks sold less because they represented a less effective topic for capturing attention and conveying the advertising message, albeit simple and localized.

The total number of advertisements found in the collection of articles that appeared in the American (and international) press in 1947 is small but significant. It is counted in the order of a few hundred pieces. It is, however, necessary to consider that at the moment, an undefined[4] percentage of the entire corpus of daily and weekly publications present in the United States in 1947 has been checked, but it can be grossly estimated at around 20-25% of the total.

4 No reliable data has been found on the number of publications in the United States in 1947. Years ago, researcher Jan Aldrich estimated (it is not known from what sources) this number to be around 10,000.

SIGN OF THE TIMES—Mrs. Olgie Ray Cordial, 333 E. Gay-st, holds the "Flying Saucer Sandwich," bacon, cheese, tomato, lettuce and mayonnaise on a bun, served on a saucer. The sandwich is the creation of Roy Tuggle, manager of the Tom Thumb Restaurant, 23 N. Third-st.

As already mentioned, advertisements related to disks, even counting articles on episodes of advertising launches of paper disks from planes, represent a sort of exception in the vast mass of ads of the time and less than 2% of the total number of 1947 clippings collected so far.

It is appropriate to present a selection of these advertisements grouped into some themes.

RESTAURANTS AND FOOD

Restaurants, bars, and commercial establishments that offered various types of food used the disks to convey their advertising messages in local newspapers, often playing on the ambiguity of the term "saucer," which indicated the concept of a small plate.

It ranged from the "steak house" to ice cream, to finally, on July 10th, the "out of this world" prices in honor of the celestial visitors to induce them to join the thousands of inhabitants of Rochester, New York, who could take advantage of the fantastic offers on meats and various cold cuts at Patty's market. The celestial visitors were invited to park their flying "Yo-Yos" on the roof (*Rochester Democrat Chronicle* July 10, 1947).

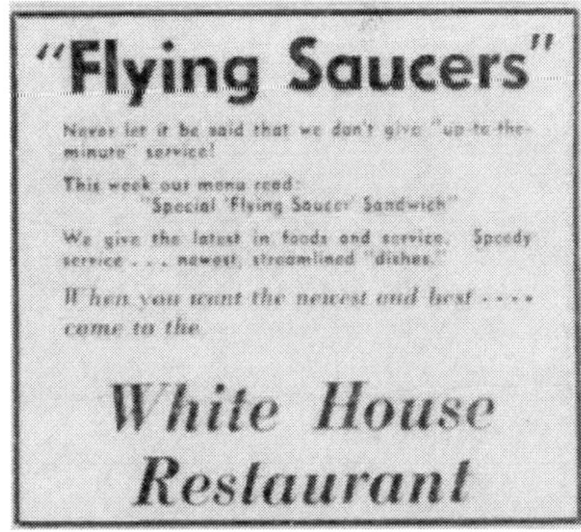

Wilmington News Journal July 11, 1947

The theme of Martians and visitors from another planet was present with a relatively high frequency in the advertisements of the time.

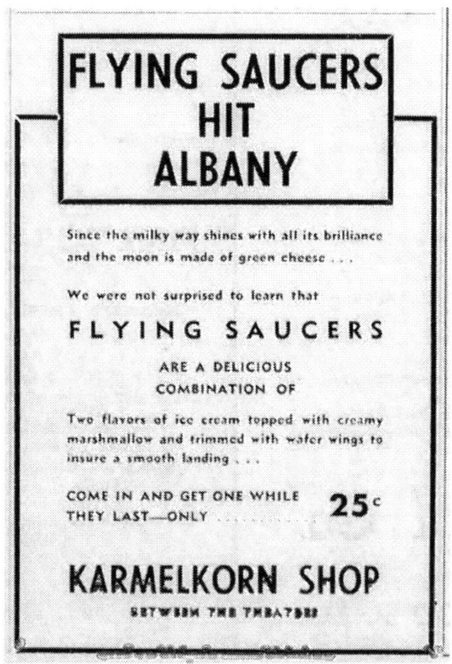

The Albany Democrat Herald July15, 1947

It certainly helped to increase the value of curiosity and wonder of the message, exploiting the idea of the technological and scientific exceptionality (therefore of the marvel and the incredible results or qualities deriving from the use of the advertised products) of the extraterrestrial visitor well present in the popular imagination of the time. The use of advertising is tangible proof, on par with the broad and relatively recurrent presence in the press articles dedicated to flying saucers.

The term "flying saucers" was usually used in the titles of advertisements to attract attention and less frequently was contextualized in the message as an integral part of it.

For example, sweets, cocktails, and sandwiches christened "flying saucers" appeared in an era that had already seen the adjective "atomic" associated with any product whose exceptional performance or prodigious qualities were to be enhanced. History repeated itself ten years later with the terms "space," “rocket,” or “Sputnik” when the population was prey to enthusiasm for the space race and the new technological marvels associated with it.

In some cases, a simple contrast was played on: for example, the ad for a grocery store in *The Billings Gazette* of July 11th contrasted flying and spinning saucers with a cascade of free-falling prices.

In the "food" sector, ice creams, probably also due to the summer season, were among the products to which most "flying saucer" advertisements were dedicated.

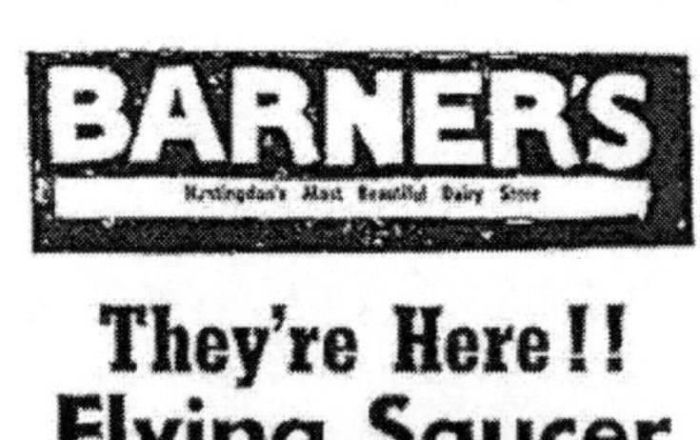

The Daily News July 15, 1947

ADVERTISEMENT

FLYING SAUCERS

If you are one of those skeptical people who don't believe in flying saucers, and you would like to see them in action, the place to go is Wimpy's. Speedy, courteous service that makes the dishes fairly fly, and man—the food that's on them! There's nothing transparent or translucent about it. Those flying plates and saucers heaped with taste-tempting goodness, food prepared by men who, through long years of experience have learned how to get the most of the best flavor out of all types of food.

Funny thing happened at Wimpy's the other day. I've heard about people who eat ketchup on everything, but I had to be shown to believe it. Mr. Hubler, the Heinz Ketchup salesman ordered a big dish of ice cream, covered it with Ketchup and ate it. Now I've seen everything. If you don't like ketchup on your ice cream we do have a delicious Spumoni Sauce, really a taste treat.

When you come to Wimpy's to see those flying plates and saucers, you can do so in cool comfort, for Wimpy's is comfortably air conditioned.

Wimpy's Steak House

1604 So. Union Phone 3-9817

Des Moines Register July 9, 1947

Brookfield Magnet July 10, 1947

Rochester Democrat Chronicle July 10, 1947

Dunkirk Evening Observer July 12, 1947

TODAY'S SPECIAL

YOU'VE HEARD ABOUT THEM —

YOU'VE SEEN THEM —

—NOW—

YOU CAN EAT THEM!

"FLYING SAUCERS"

(FULL OF NUTS)
SPECIAL TODAY …… **45c**

Hilbert's *DeLuxe* Bakery

The Logansport Press July 11, 1947

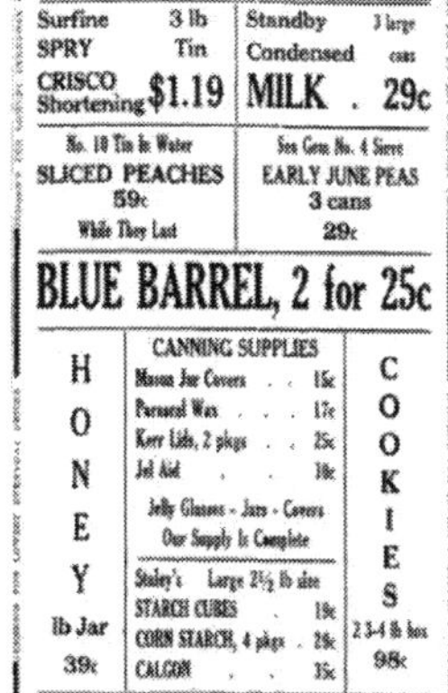

The Graettinger Times July 10, 1947

Daily News July 15, 1947

The Billings Gazette July 10, 1947

The Parma Review July 10, 1947

CARS AND OTHER PRODUCTS

Cars, motorcycles, gas stations, and auto parts stores, all the way to vacuum cleaner sellers, were the subject of advertisements that used "flying saucers" as the main eye-catching element. On July 20, a Texas newspaper had a big ad with the flashy title "Jack Carter solves the mystery of the flying saucers," with six flying saucers flying one after the other. Carter owned a company of the same name that sold hubcaps.

FLYING SAUCERS?
NOPE!
BUT WE'VE GOT
SUNOCO DYNAFUEL GAS
Don's Service Station
WILL BE OPEN EVENINGS FOR YOUR CONVENIENCE
D. R. JONES, Mgr

Chateaugay Record and Franklin County Democrat July 11, 1947

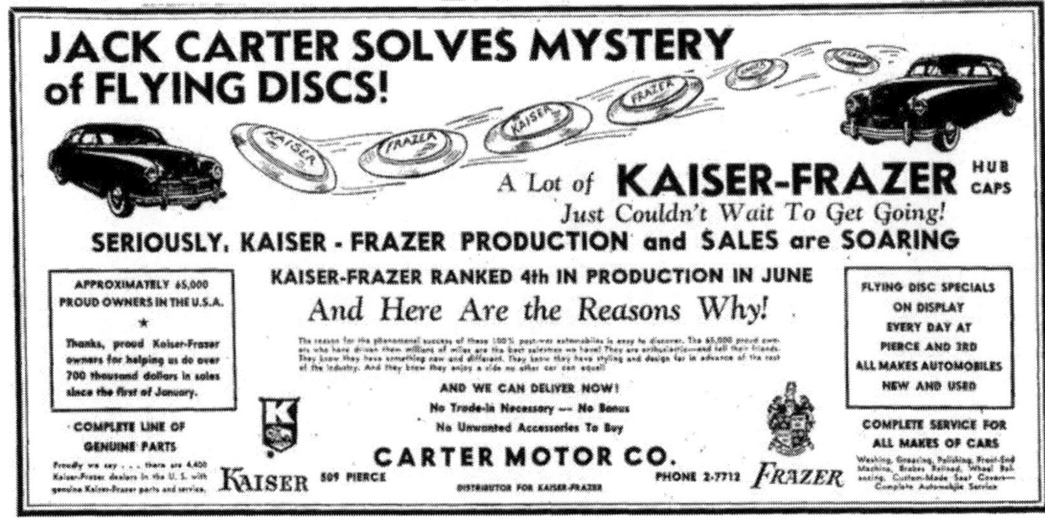

The Amarillo Sunday News Globe July 20, 1947

Nope! We Don't Have Any

FLYING SAUCERS!

BUT we do have the best values in town in our Hardware Dept. Hop on a "flying saucer" and breeze down to see our "down to earth" values.

MERVIS'

FURNITURE – HARDWARE

Hardware Dept.

Daily Courier July 10, 1947

FLYING SAUCER SPECIALS

1947

Hudson Commodore 4 door sedan with trunk, air foam cushions, Southwind heater, upholstery trimmed in blue leather. A beautiful two-tone blue, white wheel rings. This car is practically new and very beautiful. Price

$1995.00

No Trade Necessary When You Buy At VETERANS AUTO SALES

1946

Buick Super 4 door sedan, trunk. Beautiful 2-tone green, air conditioned, radio, heater, dual spot lights. A car to be proud of. Price

$2595.00

1947 Hudson Club Coupe, radio and heater
1946 Ford Super Deluxe Tudor, heater
1946 Ford Deluxe Tudor, heater
1946 Ford Deluxe Tudor, heater
1941 Chevrolet 2 door sedan, heater
1941 Chevrolet 2 door sedan, heater

MORE CARS WANTED

TOP PRICES PAID

OUR CUSTOMERS RECOMMEND US

VETERANS AUTO SALES

[illegible] GALLIA ST. PHONE [illegible]

Portsmouth Times July 18, 1947

Lewiston Daily Tribune July 10, 1947

Freeport Journal Standard July 14, 1947

The Hartford Courant July 15, 1947

FLYING SAUCERS . . . FREE!
and
GOOD TRANSPORTATION . .
WITH

No down payment

We have Central New York's largest stock of Motor Scooters, Motorbikes, and Powercycles . . . all guaranteed to give you a safe, economical ride. Such famous names as Servi-Cycle, LaRay and Comet are available to you now.

FLYING SAUCER SPECIAL!

- RIDE TO WORK—it's a great feeling to be able to come and go when you want to
- RIDE TO SCHOOL — and carry your books in the compartment provided
- RIDE TO SHOP—busy housewives are finding motorscooter shopping quick and easy
- RIDE FOR FUN—plenty of sunshine and fresh air—organize a scooter club

LaRay and Servi-Cycle MOTOR BIKES from $210 | COMET SCOOTERS from $163

SEE THEM and RIDE THEM at **BAILEY MARINE CORP.**

573 E. GENESEE ST — CORNER OF McBRIDE

Syracuse Herald Tribune July 10, 1947

Democrat and Chronicle July 16,1947

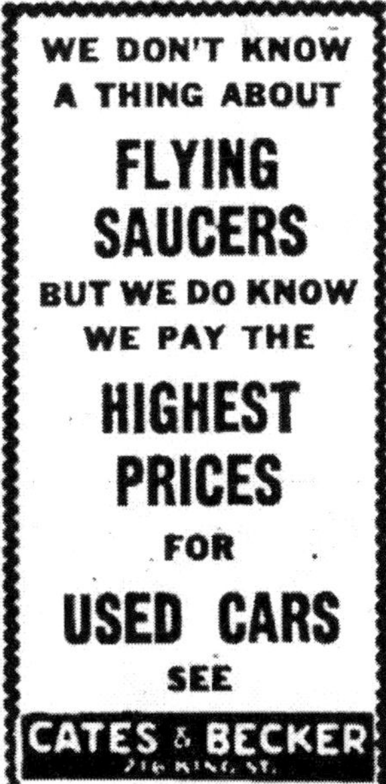

Pottstown Mercuy July 23, 1947

Walla Walla Union Bulletin July 10, 1947

Wichita Daily Times July 17, 1947

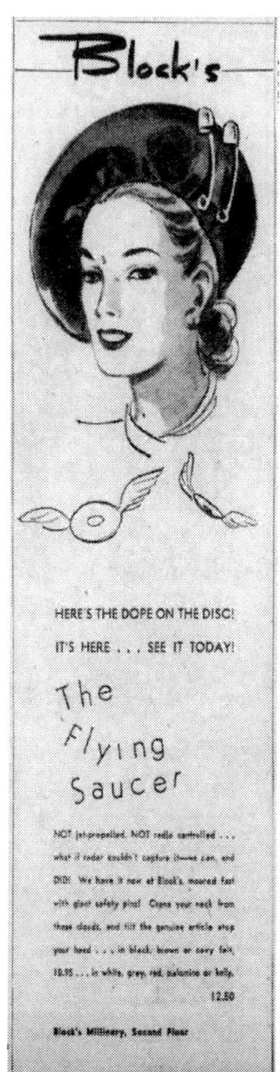

The Indianapolis Star July 11, 1947

Denton Record Chronicle July 17, 1947

Democrat and Chronicle July 15, 1947

The Troy Times Record July 23, 1947

ECONOMIC ANNOUNCEMENTS

Even the Man From Mars Can See This Bargain

5-Room brick, living room with fireplace, dining room, kitchen with plenty of cabinets, tiled drain, 2 large bedrooms, 1 bedroom 14x28, floor furnace. Stairs to attic storage. Textoned, tiled bath, shower. On Amherst handy to Inwood shopping center. Would GI with $... Total price $10,800. Mr. Alger, L-2108.

C. C. McLAIN

4017 Cedar Springs.

Dallas Morning News February 8, 1947

The so-called "economic announcements" that crowded entire pages of newspapers, printed in small, hard-to-read characters, were a popular, low-cost advertising tool. Unfortunately, the use of small text sizes and low-quality scans have made automatic character recognition (OCR) problematic. This is the basis for processing scans of old newspaper pages to allow computer searches. It is reasonable to think that only a part of the economic announcements published in the digitized newspapers of the time can actually be reached through electronic searches.

FLYING SAUCERS

may be seen from this nice suburban home as there is a beautiful unobstructed view clear to Camelback and Squaw Peak. Six miles NW, on paved street, this clean, neat and comfortable, nicely furnished, 2-bedroom and sleeping porch home is offered for a quick sale. 5½ acres with street frontage of 367 feet. A smart buy for only $11,900, with terms. See Mr. Benjamin for details.

Arizona Republic July 8, 1947

FLYING SAUCERS

EXPLAINED

G. I. wives get angry with veteran husbands who have not yet selected one of our 30 homes—NO CASH DOWN.

HOMES, Inc., 40 Hunt St., Newton Corner, or HOMES, Inc., 294 Wash. St., Boston (Rm. 310)

Daily Boston Globe July 9, 1947

Most of these text-only ads, whose highlighting was usually represented by the wording "flying saucers," were aimed at advertising real estate or cars. For example, in an Arizona newspaper on July 8, a house was presented in a suburban area from which flying saucers could be seen. It was a really great added value for the property and the lucky buyers!

FLYING SAUCERS

Whizzing cars! Some from L. A., some from Mars? They've got to sleep, these chauffeur guys. Investigate our Motel buys. From $32,000 up, we specialize. RALPH REALTY, 4134 El Cajon, R-2574

San Diego Union July 8, 1947

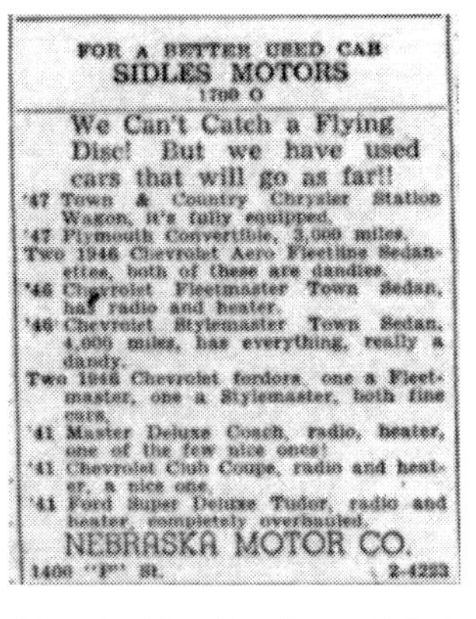

FOR A BETTER USED CAR

SIDLES MOTORS

1700 O

We Can't Catch a Flying Disc! But we have used cars that will go as far!!

'47 Town & Country Chrysler Station Wagon, it's fully equipped.

'47 Plymouth Convertible, 3,000 miles.

Two 1946 Chevrolet Aero Fleetline Sedanettes, both of these are dandies.

'46 Chevrolet Fleetmaster Town Sedan, has radio and heater.

'46 Chevrolet Stylemaster Town Sedan, 4,000 miles, has everything, really a dandy.

Two 1946 Chevrolet fordors, one a Fleetmaster, one a Stylemaster, both fine cars.

'41 Master Deluxe Coach, radio, heater, one of the few nice ones!

'41 Chevrolet Club Coupe, radio and heater, a nice one.

'41 Ford Super Deluxe Tudor, radio and heater, completely overhauled.

NEBRASKA MOTOR CO.

1400 "P" St. 2-4233

Lincoln Evening Journal July 11, 1947

THE ABILENE, TEXAS, REPORTER-NEWS

Page 18 Sunday Morning, July 13, 1947

CLASSIFIED DISPLAY

JULY USED CAR SALE

Must Reduce Our Inventory

Free Flying Saucer With Every Car Purchased First Week of Sale

COME EARLY!

46 Chevrolet ½ ton Panel. 3,000 actual miles.

42 Chevrolet 2 door Sedan. Radio. Very clean.

42 DeSoto club coupe. Radio, heater. A beauty.

41 Chevrolet coupe. Radio, heater, good tires.

41 Studebaker Champion Club Coupe. Radio. Heater. Nice Car.

41 Ford one ton Panel. Excellent condition. Bargain price.

41 Chevrolet Special Deluxe 2 door Sedan. Radio, heater, spot and fog lights. Low mileage.

40 Ford deluxe coupe. Radio, heater. Auxiliary seats. Spot light. Fender guards.

40 Chrysler New Yorker Sedan. Fully Equipped.

40 Mercury 2 door. Extra clean.

39 Plymouth coupe. Smooth motor. Good rubber. Nice looking.

38 Ford 2 door. Good car with good tires.

38 Plymouth Deluxe 4 door. Radio. Attractive.

38 Chevrolet Deluxe coupe. Good tires. Radio.

37 Dodge 4 door. New throughout.

THE BIG LOT

617 Pine Street

In the Heart of Used Car Row

Abilene Reporter News July 13, 1947

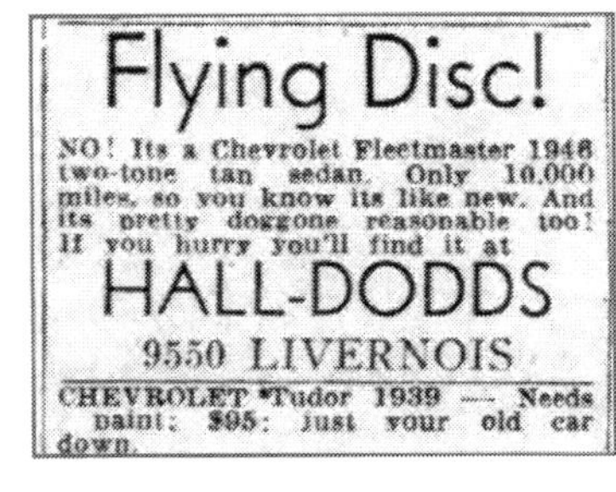

Flying Disc!

NO! Its a Chevrolet Fleetmaster 1946 two-tone tan sedan. Only 10,000 miles, so you know its like new. And its pretty doggone reasonable too! If you hurry you'll find it at

HALL-DODDS

9550 LIVERNOIS

CHEVROLET Tudor 1939 — Needs paint; $95; just your old car down.

Detroit Free Press July 12, 1947

The title represented the advertiser's choice to make the ad stand out to a reader who had to pick through dozens of virtually identical messages. In those days, flying saucers represented a kind of magnet capable of catalyzing the attention and curiosity of many people. The texts' tone was usually playful to convey the advertising message even more immediately and popularly.

MISCELLANEOUS

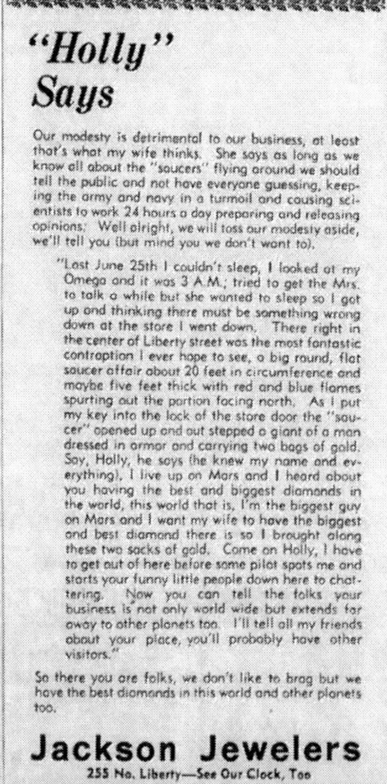

Daily Capital Journal July 12, 1947

Some advertisements presented by American newspapers in July 1947 were aimed at promoting many other products or services, including gas stations, paints, toys, airplane flights, beds, music records, movies, insurance, jewelry, stockings, housewares, plates and glasses, electric utility services, sermons by reverends of various denominations, personal loans, coal, advertising agencies, banks, opticians, real estate.

As mentioned, only a minority of the local daily (and weekly) newspapers published in the United States in the summer of 1947 have been checked so far. This, like the sightings on the territory, determines a completely partial, at least quantitative, knowledge of what was actually produced with advertising messages.

In any case, I believe that what is available today probably represents a sample that is sufficiently significant and capable of appreciating, in its general lines, the immediate impact that flying saucers had on the popular communication tool represented by advertising announcements.

A curious text ad was published on July 12 to promote a jeweler. In it, a short fictional story was described, anticipating, by a few years, situations that would become typical of the most classic UFO cases. The text is worth reproducing:

> *Last June 25th I couldn't sleep. I looked at my Omega and it was three in the morning; I tried to talk a little with my wife, but she wanted to sleep, so I got up and thinking there was some problem down at the shop, I went down. Right in the middle of Liberty Street there was the most fantastic gadget I could ever hope to see, a big round flat disk, almost seven meters in circumference and perhaps just under two meters thick, with red and blue flames coming out of the north side. As soon as I put the keys in the shop door the disk opened and a giant man jumped out wearing armor and carrying two bags of gold. Holly, he tells me (he knew my name and everything), I live on Mars and I heard you have the most beautiful and largest diamonds in the world, this world that is, I'm the biggest guy on Mars and I want my wife to have the best and biggest diamond there, so I brought these two sacks of gold. Come on Holly, I have to get out of here before some pilot sees me here and starts chattering with your little funny people. Now you can tell your friends your business is not only worldwide but extends far beyond to other planets too. I'll tell all my friends about your place, you'll probably get more visits.*

A rare example of a large and prominent advertising message based on the idea of flying saucers was the one published by a New Mexico newspaper on July 14 (six days after the first news of the Roswell recovery, which occurred in the same state). A whole page was even dedicated to eleven advertisers gathered under a well-highlighted heading entitled "The mystery of the flying saucers." In a couple of these ads, the Martian concept appeared again, denied or proposed, associated with the origin of the disks.

Advertisements were also publicized for newsreel screenings containing footage about flying saucers. For example, the California *Long Beach Independent* newspaper on July 10 announced footage of the nationwide flying disk hunt by planes.

Among the most curious ads were those by preachers of some religious denominations promoting their sermons to attract more and more faithful to their functions. On July 12, the *Los Angeles Times*, for example, announced one entitled "What are the flying saucers? It's later than you think!"

The same day, a larger one was published in *The Gastonia Gazette*: the topic was "Flying Saucers - What are they?" and it was presented by none other than... Neil Armstrong, the namesake of the future first man on the moon.

Long Beach Independent July 10, 1947

Waukesha Daily Freeman July 11, 1947

The Oakland Tribune July 14, 1947

The Parma Review July 10, 1947

The Washington Post July 13, 1947

Los Angeles Times July 12, 1947

The Post Standard July 10, 1947

The Pulaski Democrat July 17, 1947

Monday, July 14, 1947 SANTA FE NEW MEXICAN Page Five

THIS VALUE IS NO HOAX!
GLADSTONE GIN
Distilled London Dry Gin
Distilled from 100% Grain
5th $2.95
CENTRAL PHARMACY
Free, Fast Motorcycle Delivery
Phone 1316

The Mystery of the FLYING SAUCERS

WE CONFESS

It Was All Just a Publicity Stunt... To Let You Know About These High-Flying Values - - - At Deep Down Prices!

The Saucers May Be "Phony" But These Values Aren't!
Rainbow Striped
OUTING FLANNEL
Regularly 36c per yard ... Yd. 25¢
NO LIMIT
(Tuesday Only)
BELL'S

"FLYING SAUCERS"?
The Gals from Mars might prefer a different costume...
But you'll like our startling bargains in dresses! Cottons and jerseys ... prints and plains ... sports frocks and dressy styles.
Regularly to $18.95 $5.95
EMPORIUM
Santa Fe's Style Center

MARTIANS OR SANTA FEANS ... MAKES NO DIFFERENCE!
They All Prefer ...
Authentic Indian Designs from Early Pueblo Pottery on Hand-Painted
Hand-Woven
WOOL TIES
Also ranch brands and the typical Santa Fe "Land of Manana" ties.
$2.50
BURRO WEAVERS
228 Don Gaspar
Phone 487

No "Men From Mars" Folks! But "Values Out of This World"
Super Specials for "Disc Day"
TUESDAY
Banana Splits 30c
Sundaes 20c
THE SWEET SHOP
222 Galisteo

No Mystery About This "Flying Saucer"
HI-HEEL PYTHON SHOE
Styled by Kimel's of California
Regularly $18.95
Only $9.97
at the
GUARANTEE

WHO SAID THE "FLYING SAUCER" IS A JOKE?
We not only have the saucers but we have cups to go with them.
Gold Band China Cup and Saucer 45c
TAICHERT'S

You'll Be "Flying High" Too, With Bargains Like These!
WEDDING SETS
Lovely 14-K Solid Gold Mountings. To Be Cherished Forever.
$25.00 and up
Hall's
JEWELRY SHOP

THESE "FLYING DISCS" ARE REALLY PHENOMENAL!
"The Five Discs"
Direct from Psychomania
Playing Their "Hysteria Polka"
Wine Served in "Saucers"
PALOMINO CLUB
CERRILLOS ROAD
Phone 2730-W

THE REPORT ON THESE "FLYING SAUCER" VALUES IS TRUE
Keep in touch with developments in the "Flying Saucer" situation with a
FARNSWORTH
CHAIRSIDE
RADIO PHONOGRAPH
$179.95
CARTWRIGHT HARDWARE
127 W. San Francisco Phone 4??

We Can't Protect Your Car From the Flying Saucers...
But we can protect it from flying rocks and gravel with an application of 3-M undercoat! Ask us for more information.
Ballew Motor Company
"Your Friendly Chrysler-Plymouth Row Dealer"

Santa Fe New Mexican July 14, 1947

Valley Morning Star July 27, 1947

The Gastonia Gazette July 12, 1947

ADVERTISING ABROAD

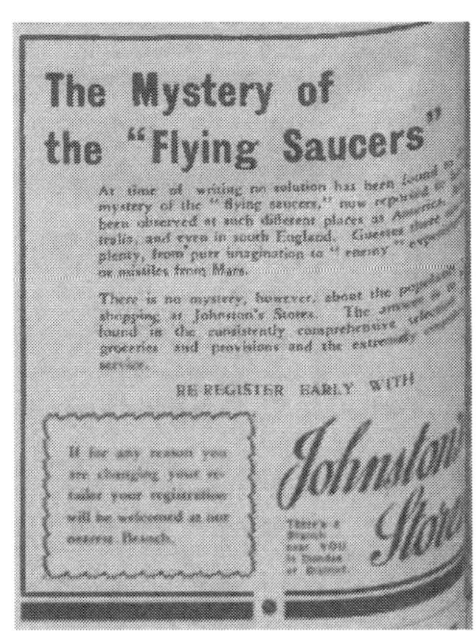

Evening Telegraph (UK) July 10, 1947

A small number of advertisements related to flying saucers have also been identified in newspapers published outside the United States. This rarity can be explained both by the considerably smaller presence of advertising inserts in these media outlets (due to a very different market and other factors: think, for example, that European newspapers of the time offered a reduced or minimal number of pages) and by the reduced possibility of systematic monitoring, still existing, for most European headlines.

A Noite (Brazil) July 21, 1947

In an ad published in the English newspaper Evening Telegraph on July 10, the "mystery of the flying saucers" was used to promote a chain of stores.

FLYING SAUCERS?

Well, your guess is as good as ours!

But let's come down to earth. You say you want security? Right. A skilled trade with a pension at the end of it? That's understandable. And a chance to see the world?

If you are the right type of man the Royal Air Force offers you these things.

Come and have a chat about your future prospects at:

R.A.F. RECRUITING CENTRE
59, High Street, Maidstone
'Phone 3798

Kent Sussex Courier (UK) August 1, 1947

Similar to what happened in previous events in the US, the advertisement featured an opening statement that emphasized the enigmatic and unclear nature of the phenomenon, along with the potential Martian origin, and contrasted it with the assurance of the commercial offer.

A Brazilian newspaper (particularly active in presenting news on the new phenomenon) illustrated the ad of a local business with a drawing, while another English newspaper used flying saucers in the title of an advertising announcement by the Royal Air Force aimed at recruiting new personnel.

PAPER PLATES

Hopes Of Getting Flying Disc Rewards Dashed

"Flying Saucers" Rain From The Sky In Daylight

Windsor Daily Star July 8, 1947

In the United States, advertising leaflets dropped from airplanes was commonplace. During the days when stories of strange sightings in the sky were spreading, the episodes in which these rains of leaflets were mistaken for the famous flying disks everyone was talking about were numerous. Today, it is hard to believe that banal episodes like dropping paper sheets from a plane could have been mistaken for flying craft that should have had advanced technology. Laughing and enjoying the idea is easy, but 1947 is a time profoundly different from ours, in which a form of strong and morbid collective desire overlapped, probably pushing the majority of the population to participate in an extraordinary event.

In any case, most of the many sightings attributable to the fall of promotional leaflets were immediately explained by the articles about them. One of the first episodes related to such aerial drops was reported in the very early days of the flying disk era: on June 28, the director of a local airport said that the sightings that had occurred in parts of Oregon were probably due to the release, at high altitude, of leaflets promoting a carnival event. The launch would also have happened on Tuesday the 24th, the same day as Arnold's sighting.

The next day in Lawton, Oklahoma, a flock of shiny flat objects reflecting sunlight was seen toward the northeast, and at the same time, airplane engines were heard: the things were leaflets dropped from a plane[5]. Many other episodes followed in the coming days.

Waterloo's "Flying Saucer"

Carl Boughton, Wagner hotel, Waterloo, shows one of the 5000 "flying saucers" with which Waterloo was bombarded Wednesday afternoon. The "saucer" actually is a nine inch paper plate reminding that the Waterloo White Hawks return home Friday night to open a six day stand. The plates were dropped from two airplanes.

Waterloo Daily Courier July 10, 1947

Already in the first days of July, someone thought to make the most of the clamor aroused by the flying saucers and the intense interest that people had in the subject, whether they believed it or not. Some pranksters merely launched standard paper plates without any particular symbol. For example, disks fluttered over house roofs on July 5 or 6 in East St. Louis, Illinois. Those collected were made of pressed white paper, just over 10 inches in diameter and with a hole about 2 inches in the center[6].

Others were more business savvy and immediately exploited the situation for their commercial activity.

The owner of a Miami restaurant bought 100 colored balloons and 100 cardboard plates on which he had the name and address of the place printed. His employees inflated the balloons, attached the plates, and released them into the sky[7].

Seen Above Is The Photograph of one of the "flying saucers" which bombarded Winona Thursday. This was recovered by alert air raid wardens and brought to The Republican-Herald office.

The Winona Republican Herald July 11, 1947

5 The Des Moines Register 29 June 1947

6 Greensboro Record July 7,1947

7 The Circleville Herald July 8,1947

SCORES OF FLYING DISKS DESCEND ON MANITOWOC

Manitowoc, Wis., July 11 [Special] —For an hour or two today many persons here thought they were seeing flying saucers by the dozens and they weren't so far wrong.

John Schuette, president of the Invincible Metal Furniture Co., an aviator and also a practical joker, bought a bundle of paper plates and had them sprayed with aluminum paint in his factory. Then he took them aloft in his plane and released them over residential sections of the city.

A few minutes later the police station, radio studio and newspaper offices were answering calls regarding the discs. In the meantime Schuette was enjoying a flight in the clouds.

Chicago Daily Tribune July 12, 1947

The launch of the plates was also often used to promote events: it was a "fashionable" tool, at that time, to convey communication. The jokesters, who took the opportunity to have fun by exploiting the ease with which many people were emotionally ready to marvel and see something strange in relatively trivial things, also knew this.

200 Flying Saucers Advertise Sept. Fiesta in Falls Church

NO CAUSE FOR ALARM—About 200 "flying saucers" were scattered over Falls Church yesterday from an airplane to publicize the town's fall fiesta, to be held September 19-21. Above, Mike Chew, 8 (left), of 300 Berry st., Falls Church, passes one of the saucers which he retrieved from a tree to his brother, Gary. Fiesta profits will help residents buy land for public park

Falls Church was bombarded by 200 "supersonic flying saucers," at 4 p. m. yesterday.

The gadgets, which strongly resembled paper plates, were scattered from a low-flying plane and bore announcements of the town's "Fiesta" September 19-20-21 to raise funds for a public park.

C. F. Blanding, chairman of the Falls Church Park Planning Committee, said the three-day fiesta would include a country fair, flower shows, street dancing, parades, athletic events, historical pageant, and a tour of local historic homes.

The paper "saucers" were scattered over Falls Church yesterday by L. R. Eskin, wartime naval flier, who lives at 408 Linden la. Chairman Blanding urged children finding the plates to save them for free fiesta tickets.

The proposed Falls Church park would cover roughly 14 acres in the Tripps Run area. It will serve primarily as a family picnic and recreation area. Some playground facilities will be set up, in addition to fireplaces, tables and swings.

The Washington Post July 17, 1947

For example, one John Schuette, president of a metal notion company near Manitowoc, Wisconsin, combined his passion for aviation with that for pranks. He bought many paper disks and painted them in his company with metallic color paint, then launched them from his private plane over some city residential areas. A few minutes later, the police station, the radio station, and the local newspaper offices were already responding to citizens' calls, reporting the presence of the disks over the city while Schuette was enjoying the joke[8].

Real Flying Saucers Fill Georgia Skies

PERRY, Ga. —(UP)— South Georgia skies from Macon to the Florida border were clouded with flying saucers—the real ones.

It was no joke. Supervisors of the Middle Western Ocmulgee River Oil Conservation District took advantage of the craze by printing on the face of each saucer this legend:

"Urge all farmers to plant blue lupine for soil improvement on land where peanuts have been harvested.

"For further information see your representatives of the Soil Conservation Service."

The appeal for use of the soil-building winter cover crop was unloaded from planes.

Abilene Reporter News September 9, 1947

In the second phase, to avoid misunderstandings or even alarms, the organizers of these advertising disk launches began to notify local newspapers, informing local communities. It was a cunning strategy that allowed advertisers to increase the launches' promotional efficacy significantly. The launches by that point were practically expected.

TOMORROW AFTERNOON

THE FLYING SAUCERS

Will Appear In The Sky Over The Twin Cities!

300 ARE LUCKY!

The News Palladium August 1, 1947

8 Chicago Daily Tribune July 12, 1947

Making the saucers popular: cartoons and comics in the 1947 press

The press has always used cartoons as a powerful way to express satire, and satire was worth for popularly important topics. Saucers were one of them in a short time span of about two weeks in early July 1947. Comics were a powerful tool to entertain people, delivering concepts and dreams from everyday life. They were still influential in the United States in 1947 when the TV was in its early infancy: many newspapers devoted nearly a full page daily, and the Sunday editions of many others hosted a great deal of comics. Those Sunday editions were the best sellers for each newspaper, often with tens of pages (while in Europe, due to the paper shortage, they had four pages or something more). Many bought a newspaper just on Sunday, and the comics pages were their favorite section, if not the main reason for the purchase.

Most but all of the many cartoons about the saucers published in 1947 were basically satirical and related to issues of those days (for example, the soaring prices of everyday life). Very few of them involved the concepts of Martians or visits from another planet. They were frequently printed on the comments and editorial pages. Occasionally, they got the privilege of being on the front page.

Many newspapers syndicated and published many cartoons, usually in a short period. The illustrators of local newspapers designed other cartoons and never left their original source. Some comics were published by foreign newspapers (or satirical weeklies in France) to be ironic towards that new weird story coming from America. Though the Americans won the war and were seen as the major world power, the United States was still perceived as the land of gullibility and strange things.

The fact that the saucers were taken as a bizarre yet worthy of attention topic is confirmed by the appearance of cartoons just two days after the nationwide publication of the Arnold sighting. Most of them depicted ground observers seeing discs flying high in the sky and usually associating them with the main concerns of people in those days, like the increase in the cost of living and taxes. Besides these and other clearly ironic cartoons (aimed at showing the saucers as nonsense and the people reporting them as nuts), more were devoted to politics and the fear of an atomic war. The flying saucers were a powerful rhetoric image, loaded with awe and amazement for the wonders of science and technology, and able to emphasize standard topics using the day's topic effectively.

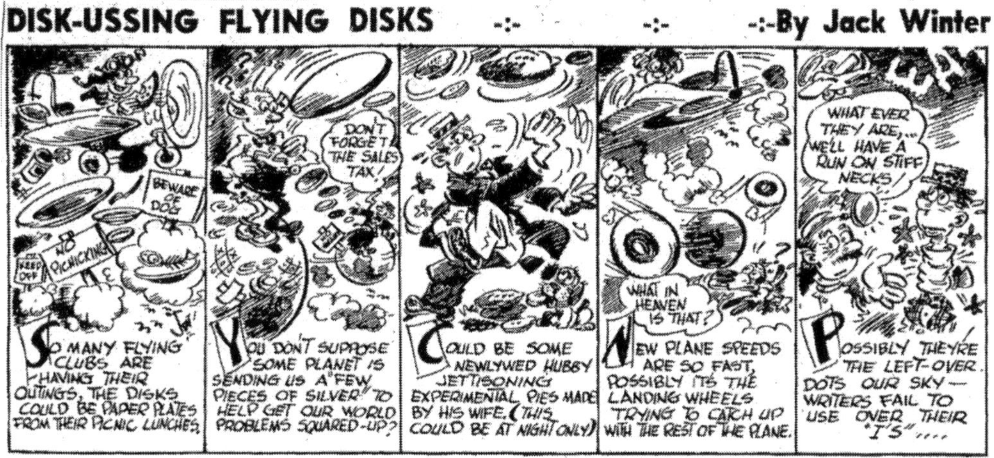

The Seattle Times June 29, 1947

The cartoons helped create the early saucer imagery: sketches and drawings by artists, though usually more detailed and visually attractive, were much rarer. Cartoonists used - ironically - the sighting descriptions from the newspapers to imagine the shape of those objects flying in the sky. Since they were named "saucers" (or "discs" or, less frequently, "disks") and that many witnesses seemed to describe them like that, they drew round objects, sometimes enriched by a sort of "holes" in their bottom part, a feature that the later saucer imagery will broadly exploit. They were usually crude and straightforward drawings just because they were used for satirical cartoons. One exception was the one published by the *East Oregonian* on July 5, depicting some crescent-shaped objects and a light airplane in the background. It was a nice reenactment of the Arnold sighting. Arnold himself used that crescent shape in his 1950 booklet.

The *Seattle Times* published one of the first cartoons in late June, portraying a sort of Martian with large ears and antennas sending "pieces of silver" to Earth to fix the world's problems. It was inside a set of four, illustrating different ironic explanations for the puzzling objects in the sky. Mars was one of those funny explanations.

The Sunday Sentinel Star July 6,1947

The extraterrestrial idea was leveraged again in the first of three funny cartoons introducing a "California occult leader" dressed as a wizard, claiming to have made contact with the flying saucers coming from another world "last November." The "occult leader" was Meade Layne, whose bizarre idea of "ether ships" coming from another dimension was quoted by several newspapers, often without even mentioning his name.

SAUCERS AS HARBINGERS OF TAXES AND HIGHER COST OF LIVING

The first newspapers offering cartoons about the brand new celestial visitors were just from Oregon, where the story originated. They were the first of a long series focusing on other popular topics: increased cost of living (food and rents above all), inflation, and taxes.

The flying saucers were depicted as a precursor of such infamous issues and were often portrayed as giant coins flying in the sky. The message looked something like "people see strange things in the sky as a consequence of their worries for their everyday life." Some cartoons ironically showed winged[9] or dollar-shaped saucers with the text "tax cut," likely suggesting the promised tax cuts were just illusions like the flying saucers.

Portland Journal June 28, 1947

The Oregonian June 28, 1947

Arizona Republic July 3, 1947

The Fresno Bee July 7, 1947

9 The flying saucers were sometimes depicted in cartoons as plates (the larger alternative to saucers) with angel wings, a clear reference to the fact that... they flew!

Cleveland Plain Dealer July 8, 1947

The Morning Sentinel July 8, 1947

Tampa Bay Times July 8, 1947

The Akron Beacon July 8, 1947

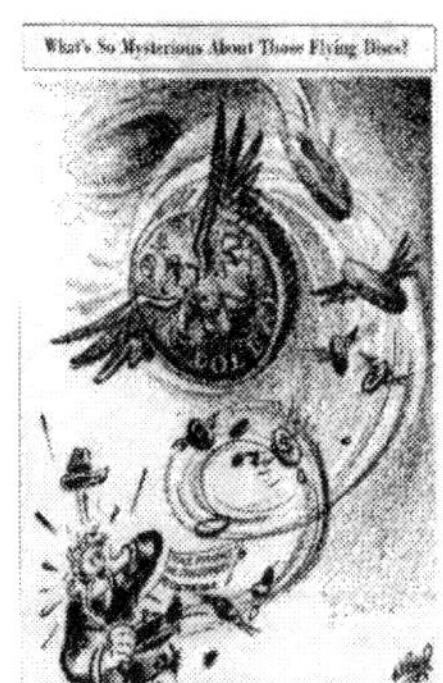

The Indianapolis Star July 8, 1947

The Tennessean July 8, 1947

Ausbury Park Press July 9, 1947

The Knickerbocker New July 9, 1947

Detroit Free Press July 10, 1947

St. Louis Post Dispatch July 10, 1947

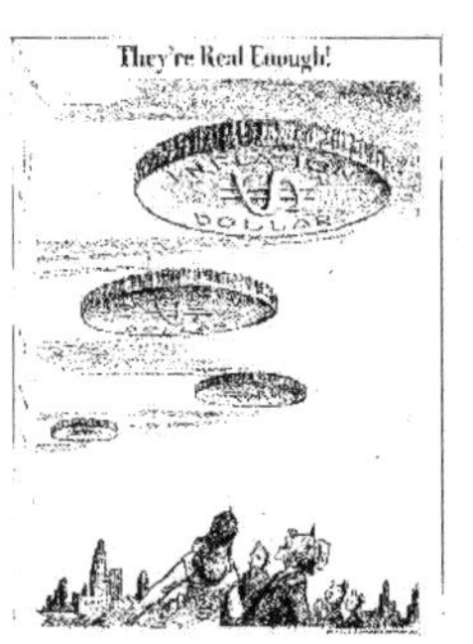

Greensboro Record July 11, 1947

The Oregonian July 12, 1947

Miami Herald July 14, 1947

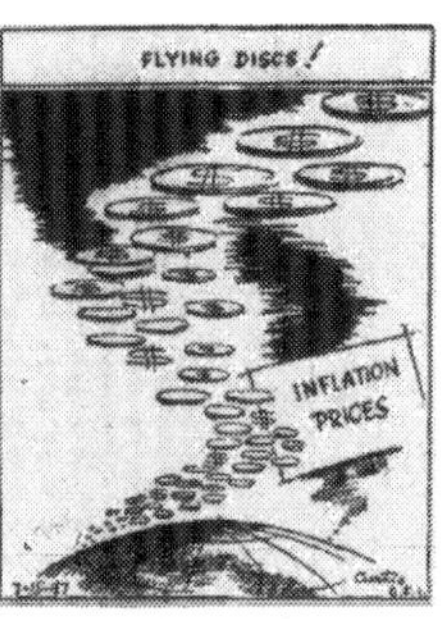

Waunakee Tribune July 17, 1947

Galveston Tribune July 18, 1947

Cedar Rapids Tribune July 24, 1947

ATOMIC COLD WAR

The shock and awe of the new atomic age and the more and more dangerous tensions with the Soviet Union were soon used to illustrate the cartoons. Atomic energy was a highly confused mix of conflicting terrific fears and great hopes based on the awareness that science fiction turned into reality out of the blue.

The atomic bomb looked like the result of extraordinary science, so many extraordinary flying saucers were associated with that same science (the press reported some rumors about the saucers as the result of experiments in mysterious "transmutation of atomic energy," immediately denied by atomic scientists). In a few cartoons, the saucers were just the result of the people's anxiety about a possible nuclear war. In contrast, in others, the mysterious objects were powerful American flying dollars seen by Stalin and the Russian bear as a threat to the communist expansion in Europe.

Pittsburgh Post Gazette

Denver Post July 7, 1947

Brooklyin Daily Eagle July 8, 1947

Minneapolis Star July 8, 1947

St. Petersburg Times July 8, 1947

The Hartford Courant July 8, 1947

The Los Angeles Times July 10, 1947

Hamilton Daily News Journal July 10,1947

Lubbock Morning Avalanche July 11, 1947

The Marion Star July 11, 1947

FRONT PAGES

Though plenty of newspapers published one or more articles on the front page of their editions between June 26 and the end of July (and a minority even devoted large or huge headlines), they just occasionally placed a cartoon in such a predominant position. When this happened, the cartoons got a generous space, though.

The percentage of foreign newspapers and weeklies publishing a cartoon on the front page was higher. Maybe this was due to their much lower number of pages: the American newspapers enjoyed more space, so a more extensive choice of content placements made their front page even richer in "important" news. This could mean that those US newspapers publishing large headlines, photographs, and cartoons on the front page considered the weight of the saucer news really relevant, at least from the point of view of their readership's interest.

Urges Speed on Opening Our Door for Displaced Persons

ONE-WAY TRAFFIC FOR DOWNTOWN ALLEYS

THE AMARILLO GLOBE

'NO MUSIC FOR RADIOS'

Sidewalk Savants Squint Skyward For Solution of Soaring Saucers

Petrillo Tells Congress He Is 'Thinking of' Ban

Pioneer Couple Dies Within 10-Hour Span

BULLETIN

Block Plan To Lease Tri-State Fair Park

Bandit Slain, Cop Wounded in Duel

The Amarillo Globe July 7, 1947

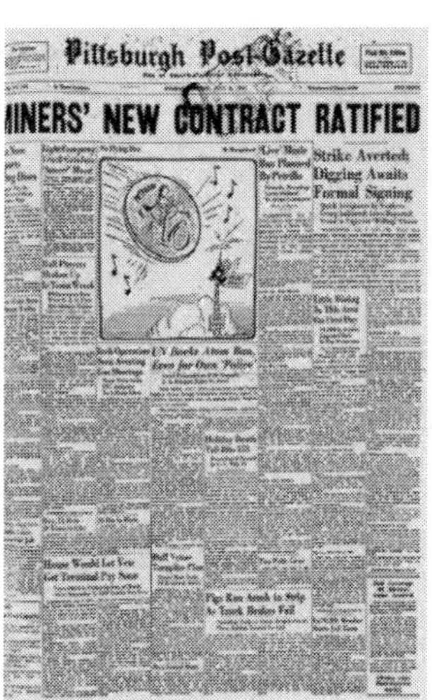

Pittsburgh Post-Gazette

INERS' NEW CONTRACT RATIFIED

Strike Averted; Digging Awaits Formal Signing

Pittsburgh Post Gazette July 8, 1947

The Coshocton Tribune

Secret A-Bomb Data Stolen From Oak Ridge, Newspaper Says

2,000 SEIZED IN GREEK ROUNDUP OF COMMUNISTS

The Coshocton Tribune July 9, 1947

SANITY HEARING CALLED FOR AX MURDERER

ARIZONA DAILY SUN

High Court Orders Singleton Retried, Blevins Murders

Williams Cop Held As Army Fugitive

Swimming Pool Work To Start

Arizona Daily Sun July 11, 1947

GOP Threatens Night Senate Session To Pass Tax Cut Bill

The Port Arthur News

16 NATIONS PRESENT AS PARLEY AT PARIS BEGINS

Greek Red Leader Asks 'Free' State

The Port Arthur News July 12, 1947

OTHER TOPICS

Other cartoons were devoted to an assortment of topics, ranging from pure irony to political satire and news of the moment.

Buffacolo Courier Express June 28, 1947

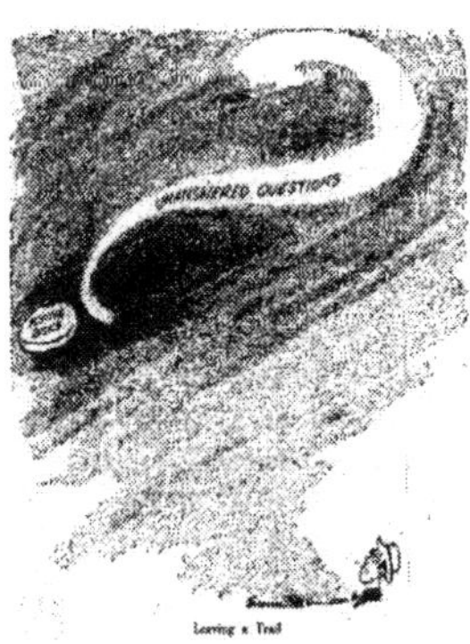

Lousiville Courier Journal July 6,1947

Boston Globe July 7, 1947

El paso Herald Post July 8, 1947

The Pittsburgh Press July 8, 1947

Flying Disk Throws Jockey

The Courier Journal July 9, 1947

The Philadelphia Enquirer July 9, 1947

Binghamton Press July 10, 1947

Delaware County Daily Times July 10, 1947

Melbourne Argus July 10, 1947

Sheboygan Press July 17, 1947

Syracuse Herald Journal July 18, 1947

Flying Saucer Out of Albany

Detroit Free Press July 20, 1947

The Daily Republican July 29, 1947

The Flying Disk

Olean Times July 24, 1947

PAPER SAUCERS EVERYWHERE

Several cartoons have been published in international newspapers since the days of the climax of the saucer wave in the United States. Most were joking and were a powerfully ironic satire against what looked like a new American mania.

It seems that all the French satirical papers, like *Le Canard Enchainé*, didn't miss the chance to be harshly ironic, each devoting one or more cartoons (as well as stories) to those new bizarre stories coming from the other side of the ocean. However, *L'Os libre* published a cartoon about the French people's hope to find food on board those celestial saucers: post-war France, like most other European countries, faced rationing and poor availabilities of food and other goods. The flying saucers were crudely drawn like plates or cups, designed even in a more straightforward style than that used by the American newspapers.

The Brazilian dailies devoted a great deal of space to the saucers in July 1947, including several front pages with huge head titles. Such great "enthusiasm" for the saucers also produced some cartoons, and a few were even published on the front pages, giving them maximum exposure to the readers.

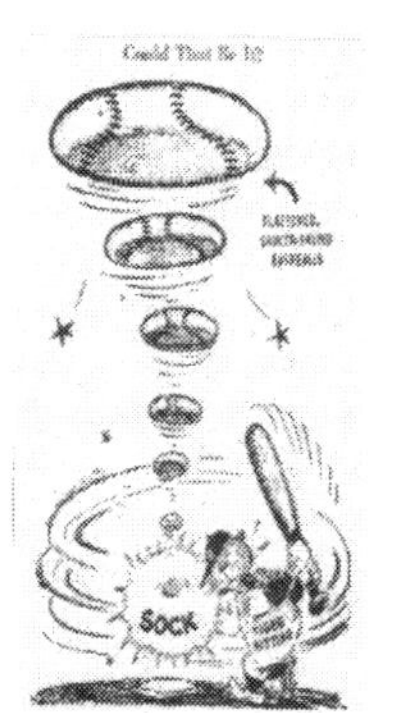

Windows Star (CAN) July 7, 1947

Berlingske Tidende (DENMARK) July 8, 1947

New Zealand Herald (NEW ZEALAND) July 8, 1947

Tumulto na Conferência Internacional do Trabalho

GAZETA DE NOTICIAS

Solução dos problemas da Europa sôbre base econômica

Gazeta de Noticias (BRAZIL) July 9, 1947

Folha da Manha (BRAZIL) July 15, 1947

GAZETA DE NOTICIAS

TREMENDA LUTA NA FRONTEIRA GRECO-ALBANESA

Navegação do Prata, no plano continental

Participação da Nicaragua na Conferência do Rio de Janeiro

Agora 'panelas-voadoras'

Gazeta de Noticias (BRAZIL) July 15, 1947

L'Os Libre (FRANCE) July 30, 1947

Guignol (FRANCE) August 8, 1947

o Malho (BRAZIL) September 1947

COMICS

The comic strips were a prevalent feature of most but all American newspapers, especially in their Sunday editions. They covered a pretty extensive range of topics and situations, including science fiction.

Los Angeles Times April 13, 1947

The reader of an Australian newspaper[10] published in Broken Hill (NSW) wrote a letter (blaming capitalism and praising socialism) to point out that flying saucers were the product of the "comic-strip age" introduced to the United States by the millionaire press, radio and motion picture monopolies. Those who controlled those industries were directly responsible for the American public's hysteria.

Sci-fi comic heroes such as Buck Rogers, Flash Gordon, Superman, and Brick Bradford had been involved in stories with fantastic spaceships and extraterrestrials (mostly martians) throughout the previous two decades. Such comics were regularly published in syndication by many newspapers in all the American states in the first half of 1947. In the Buck Rogers strips, which were definitely the most popular at the time, spaceships were rocket-shaped, but after the summer wave, some became flying saucers.

A highly popular topic like the saucers could not miss the comic strips, though this started to happen a few weeks after the top of the wave. It seems another clue of how the flying saucers had quickly become a component of modern popular culture and still are after over seven decades.

---

10 Barrier Miner July 10,1947

The first mention of flying saucers in a comic strip seems to have been published on July 23 by several newspapers, just a few days after the end of the overwhelming wave. It was just a quick mention about the furor of the saucers in the news, with no other link.

Asbury Park Press July 28, 1947

A few days later, another strip used the flying saucers for a funny joke: a kid breaking a set of dishes announced to his grandma that "some flying saucers in loose formation just landed in our kitchen." A large number of newspapers syndicated the strip.

The Clarion Ledger July 29, 1947

Another ironic comic strip was published the day after, once more joking about the double meaning of flying saucers, both mysterious flying objects in the sky and everyday dishes available in the homes of all families.

Another fun comic strip was released at the beginning of October.

Tallahassee Democrat October 5, 1947

The Morning News August 21, 1947

Some newspapers, including the *Baltimore Sun* and the *Philadelphia Sunday Bulletin*, published an 8-page color insert comic book in late September. It was "The Spirit" franchise by Will Eisner, and that story is usually credited as the first one entirely devoted to the flying saucer theme (seemingly linking it with Mars).

Philadelphia Sunday Bulletin September 28, 1947

Another funny comic strip was published in early October.

In November, issue 48 of the *Startling Comics* magazine included a 2-page article titled "The man-killer on Mars" with a lovely illustration depicting three flying discs.

The most exciting exploitation of flying saucers in the (science fiction) comics is about the Buck Rogers strips, starting in early September.

Startling Comics November 1947

Buck Rogers was originally a space opera character created by Philis Francis Nowlan in the novella Armageddon 2419 A.D. and then adapted in a comic strip designed by Dick Calkins (1895-1962), published for the first time in a newspaper on January 7, 1929, as "Buk Rogers in the 25th Century A.D.". Buck Rogers became an important part of American pop culture, ranging from comic strips to movies, radio, and television. Calkins was the very first artist to draw the Buck Rogers strips until November 1947.

Perhaps Phil Nowlan and Dick Calkins could be credited with the idea and cartooned version of the flying saucer much earlier in the Buck Rogers strip. Between 1929 and 1947, the hero was associated with an extensive range of spaceships: though most of them were rocket-shaped and clearly reflected the mainstream imagery of the time for a space vessel, some of them were

Examples of saucer-shaped spacecraft featured in the Buck Rogers comic strips, before Arnold.

unusually shaped, including some domed saucers with portholes, of striking resemblance with later saucer iconography. The strips were regularly published in syndication by hundreds of newspapers throughout the United States, making the character a hugely popular hit.

August 1938

Buck Rogers was frequently used as a rethoric icon to highlight something technologically so advanced to appear nearly out of this world, yet hard to believe. In an *Associated Press* dispatch published by several newspapers on July 1[11], some Army officials at Fort Worth were quoted saying that the discs were "Buck Rogers stuff."

One week later, other newspapers reported the funny claims of Dick Calkins, the designer of comic strips, using titles such as *DISKS? JUST BUCK ROGERS TESTING*.

Calkins seemingly telegraphed from Chicago to some newspapers this text:

> *To spare this great nation any further worry, I feel I should explain the flying disks are only part of a routine experiment I am conducting on this planet and others in connection with Buck Rogers. I feel your readers are entitled to any comfort they can get from this explanation.*[12]

The Buck Rogers strips quickly leveraged the popularity of the discs. Their first mention seems to be published on July 30. A character in the strip says:

> *Huer was experimenting with "silent noise," a new government flying disc project – and it blew up in his face.*[13]

---

[11] The Waco News Tribune, Fort Worth Star Telegram July 1, 1947

[12] Seattle Daily Times, The Bakersfield Californian, The Morning News, The San Mateo Times, The Daily Argus Leader, Oakland Tribune July 8,1947

[13] The Morning News July 30, 1947; San Mateo Times August 6, 1947

A few days later[14], the discs landed visually on the Buck Rogers strips, and Calkins began to draw them. Between early September and the end of the year, there were three series of strips at least involving flying saucers. In each series, the disks (as they were named) had a different peculiar shape.

The first was a plate with a short upper and lower cylindrical protuberance. The disks were from a "spirit world" visited by Buck Rogers, and he recalled the saucer had been seen five centuries before when the papers were full of stories about them, and all went completely nuts[15]. The flying saucers were invented by a ghost named Archimedes in that spirit world. When ghosts had to run down to Earth to haunt houses, they used flying disks, as Buck Rogers used rocket ships. He then even flew one of them.

[14] It appears that the first comic strips were published on September 5 by The Long Beach Independent and The Harrisburg Telegraph, then followed by other newspapers, including The San Mateo Times (September 12).

[15] The Harrisburg Telegraph September 29, 1947

Strips were published between September and October 1947 by various newspapers, for example, *The Harrisburg Telegraph,* between September 5 and October 13.

The second shape was a sort of heavily flattened sphere with a round hatch and evenly spaced portholes on a band placed around its circumference: it appeared between late November and early December. In a later strip[16], it became even more classic: a nearly perfect sphere (with a long, narrow window) and a thin disc with portholes placed in its middle. Such a "space disk" had been made for Buck Rogers by the ghost scientists of the spirit world, and it was controlled by telepathy.

[16] The Morning News December 2, 1947 and December 4, 1947

The third one (appearing in early December) looked like an evolution of the later version of shape two, becoming a classic flying saucer predating most of the classic saucer imagery that became popular in the 1950s. It was a large thin disc with portholes, well balanced in proportions, with a large dome and an antenna on top of it, plus a large lower protuberance.

In some strips, the dome had some windows, too. In another, the saucer was designed with a view from beneath. At the bottom of the lower protuberance were three dark spots, something pretty reminiscent of the three landing balls of the later infamous Adamski scout ship.

The strips were syndicated daily in many newspapers, though with different timings. These designs were striking prototypes of the classic saucer iconography that quickly became a primary component of modern popular culture.

Though some newspapers occasionally published art drawings of saucers, people were supposed to imagine the shape and visual features of those fantastic crafts. Also, thanks to the comic strips, this changed dramatically.

A vast number of people, many of them avid readers of the comic strips, began to be exposed to the imagery of the flying saucers for the very first time, for several days but weeks. They finally saw they were round and had a dome and portholes. These features soon became the stereotype of the classic flying saucer image that was quickly and powerfully encapsulated into popular culture. And it is still there.

The Buck Rogers strips significantly contributed to creating the flying saucer as we know it. Then the cinema (starting with minor productions such as *DAREDEVIL OF THE SKIES* in 1949 and *THE FLYING SAUCER* in 1950 and then with blockbuster hits such as *THE DAY THE EARTH STOOD STILL* in 1951) helped even more people worldwide to see and finally learn about the saucers. Calkins likely created the discs in his strips by merging the descriptions of the July sightings he read in the newspapers with some dose of fancy and previous imagery of spaceships, producing a structured "prototype" of the flying saucer that was rarely depicted in the press of 1947. Most drawings were just funny cartoons.

Though their circulation had been usually pretty limited, many artworks portraying domed disc-shaped spaceships were published in sci-fi magazines decades before 1947. One from *Amazing Stories* of July 1943 is strikingly similar to the "flying disk" shooting down enemy crafts in one of the last Buck Rogers strips in December 1947.

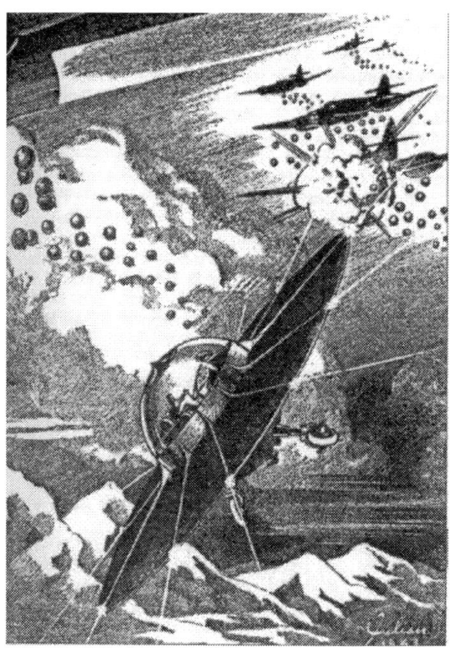

Amazing Stories July 1943

Buck Rogers was previously involved with saucer-shaped spaceships when they were not known as "flying saucers," and they didn't harass people in the United States and other countries. Other comic superheroes, like Flash Gordon, had a similar involvement in the 1930s. For example, you can easily see a classic domed flying saucer in a 1936 set of trading cards.

In a Sunday edition of the *Syracuse Herald*[17] published in 1936, the color comic strips of Buck Rogers hosted saucer-shaped spaceships with a large dome enriched by portholes and a large opening in the bottom part. In 1947, Buck Rogers was not new with the flying saucers.

Amazing Stories May 1944

In a nutshell, cartoons and comic strips helped the visual concept of the flying saucer to get known to millions of people, pushing its basic image deep into the popular culture of the time so deeply that it remained there forever. However, it changed a bit throughout the decades.

17 Syracuse Herald November 1, 1936

1947: the Boyle abduction and other encounter stories

Hal Boyle

Harold Vincent Boyle (1911-1974) was a Pulitzer Prize-winning journalist for the *Associated Press*. He was well-known as a war correspondent during World War II, and his articles were syndicated in over 700 newspapers. After the war, Boyle settled in New York and began turning out a daily column, interrupted only by further correspondent work in Korea and Vietnam.

Boyle's syndicated story of his funny abduction aboard a flying saucer from Mars piloted by an 8-foot tall green Martian was published in a very large number of American newspapers (somebody estimated over 1,000) on July 8, then often reprinted and expanded the next day. His tale was like comparable items printed by the American Yellow Press during the 1897 airship scare. This purported to be from a manuscript found in an empty beer bottle and "apparently ... fallen from a great height."

Though the saucers have been related to Mars or another unknown planet well before July 9 (actually starting on June 26), the Boyle yarn had a huge visibility impact. It reached millions of US readers, telling them that it was a ridiculous story but encapsulating into their knowledge and memory the concept that those bizarre saucers could be fantastic, highly advanced flying machines from elsewhere. From where? Throughout the previous 70 years, Mars was nearly the only planet thought to be inhabited by intelligent people.

There has been news about lights from Mars, alleged radio messages, attempts to send optical or radio signals to our civilized neighbors, earthlings claiming to be in contact with Martians or to have visited the red planet with their astral body, a vast literature of science fiction novels, books and magazines describing voyages to and from Mars, comics heroes fighting evil Martian invaders, Mars people shown in comedies and motion pictures, an infamous radio broadcast about the invasion of super-advanced Martians that was reportedly taken for real by a few millions of Americans.

It was likely that a seemingly highly technological phenomenon, something flying with unusual and superior performances and shapes, could have an exotic origin (as an alternative to more mundane explanations, the favorite choice of most commentators, intellectuals, and scientists).

A secret super-weapon was a reliable candidate. However, Mars was a fantastic alternative, authorized by many decades of popular culture suggesting that Martians were real and more advanced than us. The concept of (possible) civilized Martians was deeply rooted in the wealth of knowledge of most people reading newspapers and books, but also likely known to most uneducated persons thanks to the oral circulation of news. Such a circulation consequently produced a gross distortion of the original concepts, but it was equally influential in pushing them deeper and deeper into modern popular culture. Boyle's piece lasted just like a feeble wheeze but demonstrated the extraterrestrial hypothesis in 1947 was sufficiently visible to merit lampooning.

For sure, his real goal was to ridicule the saucer stories and the people behind them, exploiting a popular theme (Martians) that was too fantastic to be true for most people and usually confined to the realm of sci-fi pulps and comics. He used the Martians because they were likely the most "reliable" of the possible funny stories to ridicule the flying saucers and debunk the craze around them. Those celestial contraptions' seemingly technologically advanced appearance and performances required an equivalent technologically advanced tale. A giant green man from Mars and his seven-story tall hat-shaped spaceship were a good choice.

Boyle's column was funny and amused the readers of hundreds of newspapers all over the United States. It made fun of Orson Welles because of his role in the infamous 1938 hoax, turning him into the target of a Martian "treasure hunt sweepstake." An even more significant emphasis on Welles was later used inside the first comics, with a story mostly centered around the flying saucers[18].

Now We Know Those Discs Are Space Ships

Hal Boyle Goes Completely 'Up in the Air' to Explain the Flying Saucer Phenomenon

By HAL BOYLE

ABOARD A FLYING SAUCER OVER PITCHER Okla (AP)—Don't tell me these flying discs are imaginary. Here I am in the middle of one, zooming around the American landscape like a boomerang.

These things aren't discs or saucers at all. They're built like a cowboy hat seven-stories tall.

The reason you folks down below have been disagreeing about the size is you haven't seen the whole thing. All you have seen is the reflection of the sides where patches of the infra-invisible paint were burned off these huge space ships as they passed too close to the sun on their way here from Mars.

Yes Mars! I am a prisoner aboard a 1947 model "flying saucer" from another planet. Let me explain:

I left the New York public library at dusk the other day and dropped into a quiet bar to wash down a warm vitamin pill with a cold bottle of beer.

Finishing it, I turned to a silent figure sitting next to me—the only other customer at the bar—and all but fainted. I saw a thing some eight feet tall, covered with thick green hair, with one eye like a hard-boiled egg in the center of his forehead, and no visible mouth at all. He was naked, his hands were three-clawed and big enough for a Brooklyn center fielder.

The green man's yolk-yellow eye burned menacing red. One hand twisted one of a series of knobs on his chest marked "slang, American," and noiseless words drifted to me:

"Scram, Mac. But take along some beer. You're going on a long ride."

Then I found myself lifted and tossed sprawling. There was the sound of a door closing and a sense of lifting rapidly into space.

I scrambled to my feet and looked out the window—its infra-invisible paint is only invisible when you look at it from the outside. Manhattan was falling away beneath us like a toy town.

"Well how do you like your first ride in a flying saucer, Orson Welles?" leered the green man. "You're on the way to a place where there are more Martians than there ever were in New Jersey."

"Look, this may be a flying saucer," I complained, "but I'm not Orson Welles. I got this high forehead from wearing a tight hat."

"Then who are you?"

"I'm his cousin Artesian Welles," I countered, "and who or what are you?"

"I'm Balmiston X-Ray O'Rune from Mars," said the green man, "and you have probably ruined my chance to win the sweepstakes."

"What sweepstakes?"

"Why the sixty thousandth centennial running of the universal Martian treasure hunt sweepstakes," crossly grunted the green man. "This time there are 500 space ships competing. To win I have to bring back twelve rare objects including Orson Welles. Now somebody will beat me. It's all your fault for looking like somebody else."

"I'll keep you as a hostage," he said. "You steer while I catch a little sleep."

So here I am wheeling this blasted flying saucer back and forth between the Bronx, Santa Fe and Seattle. I have scribbled down this story to smuggle it out in a bottle through the gravity exhaust tube.

"Look out below, Peoria!"

RIVERSIDE STORE SOLD

Mr., Mrs. H. E. Doud New Proprietors of

REPORT POLIO CASE

DES MOINES (AP) — The first case of infantile paralysis here since June 10 was reported today by the city health department. The patient is Larry Gillespie 6. It is the third case in the city since April 1.

Iowa City Press Citizen July 8, 1947

---

18 Philadelphia Sunday Bulletin September 28, 1947

The very first article was published on July 8, and the day after, a second one was printed by most newspapers that published the first. A few other papers published the article(s) between July 10 and 11. So far, more than 100 newspapers are known to have posted those articles even on their front page, mainly on July 8, with usually attractive headlines. About 30% of all of the known Boyle's columns had the word "Mars" (or much more rarely "other planet") in their headlines[19], usually to emphasize the origin of the saucer or the pilot. Though Boyle's story was clearly ridiculous, likely, many people acquired again the concept that the saucer could be just hot air … but maybe also spaceships coming from Mars!

SPECIAL CARRIER DELIVERY SERVICE
PHONE 1148-W

The Daily Times Herald

Carroll, Iowa, Tuesday, July 8, 1947 — Eight Pages

Flying Discs Imaginary? Don't Tell Boyle--He's In One On Way to Mars!

Lewis, Operators Sign; Avert Coal Strike

The Daily Times Herald July 8, 1947

A few titles misled people to believe that a reporter was somehow involved in the saucer mystery, but most were manifestly ironic and amusing. Some newspapers printed the stories, randomly cutting sentences or even paragraphs of the original text, likely to fit the available space on their page. The complete text of his first article should read like this:

> *EDITOR'S NOTE: The following manuscript by Hal Boyle, who was last seen two days ago, reading a copy of "Tom Swift" on the steps of the New York Public Library, was found in a bottle in a perambulator in Central Park. The bottle apparently had fallen from a great height.*
> *By HAL BOYLE*
> *Associated Press Staff Writer*
>
> *Aboard a flying saucer over Pitcher, Okla. – Don't tell me these flying discs are imaginary. Here I am in the middle of one, zooming around the American landscape like a boomerang.*
> *These things aren't discs or saucers at all. They're built like a cowboy hat seven stories tall.*

19 Binghamton Press July 9, 1947; The Advocate July 10, 1947

The reason you folks down below have been disagreeing about the size is you haven't seen the whole thing. All you have seen is the reflection of the sides where patches of the infra-invisible paint were burned off these huge space ships as they passed too close to the sun on their way here from Mars.

YES, MARS!

Yes, Mars! I am a prisoner aboard a 1947 model "flying saucer" from another planet. Let me explain:

I left the New York Public Library at dusk the other day and dropped into a quiet place to wash down a warm vitamin pill.

Finishing it, I turned to a silent figure sitting next me – the only other customer in the place – and all but fainted. I saw a thing some eight feet tall, covered with thick green hair, with one eye like a hard-boiled egg in the center of his forehead, and no visible mouth at all. He was naked, his hands were three- clawed and big enough for a Brooklyn center fielder.

The green man's yolk-yellow eye burned menacingly red. One hand twisted one of a series of knobs on his chest marked "slang, American" and noiseless words drifted to me:

"Scram, Mac. You're going on a long ride."

ON HIS WAY

Then I found myself lifted and tossed sprawling. There was the sound of a door closing and a sense of lifting rapidly into space.

I scrambled to my feet and looked out the window – its infrainvisible paint is only invisible when you look at it from the outside. Manhattan was falling away beneath us like a toy town.

"Well, how do you like your first ride in a flying saucer, Orson Welles?" leered the green man. "You're on the way to a place where there are more Martians than there ever were in New Jersey."

"Look, this may be a flying saucer," I complained, "but I'm not Orson Welles. I got this high forehead from wearing a tight hat."

"Then who are you?"

"I'm his cousin. Artesian Welles," I countered, "and who or what are you?"

"I'm Balmiston X-Ray O'Rune from Mars," said the green man, "and you have probably ruined my chances to win the sweepstakes."

"What sweepstake?"

"Why the 60,000th centennial running of the Universal Martian Treasury Hunt Sweepstake!" crossly grunted the green man.

"This time there are 500 space ships competing. To win I have to bring back 12 rare objects, including Orson Welles. Now somebody will beat me. It's all your fault for looking like somebody else."

He tossed some peanuts on top of his head. To my mild surprise it opened and a double row of teeth chomped down on the peanuts. Now I know where his voice had been coming from.

"What are the other items on your treasure hunt list?" I asked.

"Oh, I've already got a slice of moon cheese, a burning spark from the sun, the fingerprint of Mother Machree, a record of Gargantua singing "Mammy," and an autographed smoke ring from Winston Churchill's cigar," said the green man.

"I've just got a few things to do in this country – like buying a new motor car, getting a good 5-cent cigar and plucking a hair from the eyebrow of John L. Lewis."

"Balmiston, old boy," I said. "I think you and the other flying saucers are going to be here a long time. Your search is only beginning."

The cartoon published together with the Boyle's story

"I'll keep you as a hostage." He said. "You steer while catch a little sleep."
So here I am wheeling this blasted flying saucer back and forth between the Bronx, Santa Fe and Seattle. I have scribbled down the story to smuggle it out in a bottle through the gravity exhaust tube. But each time the green man woke up and caught me.
Somehow I'll manage to get the bottle out. You must believe what it contains. Bigger tales than this have come out of smaller bottles.
If I succeed I'll send out more details on the flying saucers tomorrow. If, however, the green man catches me again, well -
"Look out below, Peoria!"

That article was often joined by a nice cartoon depicting Boyle's story, with the cowboy hat-shaped spaceship and the one-eyed Martian.
Then came the second article:

EDITOR'S NOTE: Our Hal Boyle, returning from a two-day absence, insists he is the first man to come back alive from a trip on a "flying saucer." You may take his story or leave it. But we are turning down his expense account for $2,880 – which is what five cents a mile comes to after 48 hours in his 1,200-mile-an-hour conveyance.
By HAL BOYLE
Associated Press Staff Writer

New York – Safe! Safe after 48 hours and 57,600 miles in a flying saucer from Mars! And now I can tell the world the full story of what happened after Balmiston X-Ray O'Rune. the eight- foot, green-haired Martian pilot, snagged me off a barstool and took me riding in a space ship.
You will remember that Balmiston – I got to calling him "Balmy" – and 499 other Martian pilots came here in flying saucers on a universe-wide "treasure hunt" sweepstakes. The game was to find and take to Mars Orson Welles and 11 other difficult objects – such as a whalebone stay from Queen Victoria's corset.
"Let's go look first for the lost gold tooth of Magellan," said Balmiston, after a few warming up trips across the continent. "We can pick up Orson Welles later."

SCATTERED CONFUSION
He poured in a fresh bottle of anti-gravity fuel, wound up the atmospheric friction-repeller. and our seven-story-high invisible flying disc whipped over the Atlantic at 20 miles a minute.
"Air trips bore me – you miss so much of the scenery," yawned Balmiston, scratching at a hangnail on his three-clawed hand.
"What would be the result if we hit the Eiffel Tower?" I worried.
"Scattered confusion," quipped Balmiston. Suddenly he grabbed the wheel from hands and spun it wildly.
"You almost ran over a jet plane, you earth dope!!" he said, but quickly apologized after I muttered:

"Okay, you backseat-driving mope from Mars. I haven't noticed you sticking out a claw on the turns."

KID SISTER, TOO

The flying saucer handled beautifully. One-eyed balmy leaned back dreamily and began to whistle through the top of his head.

"I think I'll take you up to Mars and introduce you to my sister. Violet Ray O'Rune," he said. "She's always complaining I never introduce her to any of my friends. She may take a liking to you. Nice girl, too."

"Does she have an eye in her forehead and green hair like you, Balmy?" I shuddered.

"Sure." he said, "do you think she's a freak like you? She's a cutie – got long eyelashes thin as a rope. She makes a good living, too, pulling a boat on one of the canals. Not that I think you're mercenary."

Appalled at the prospect, I began throwing bottles of anti-gravity fuel out the exhaust every time Balmy's attention wandered. As we passed over Austria, the big green man queried nervously:

"You're not cutting across Russia. are you?"

"Why not?"

"You know how touchy Stalin is about passports." said Balmy. "I don't want to start any intra-universal incident. Swing down to Egypt."

There we found Magellan's gold tooth in a Cairo curio shop. O'Rune fliched it without payment after rubbing himself with a jar of invisible cold cream.

On the way back our flying saucer began to lose altitude.

"We are running low on fuel." Said the startled green man. "I'll have to contact one of the other saucers from Mars and borrow some."

He put on the headphones of the flying disc interstellar mental telepathy radio - which I had already thoughtfully jammed.

"All I get is a broadcast from the United Nations." complained the Martian. "A man with a Russian accent keeps saying, No! no! no!"

As we settled invisibly down on Brooklyn, I took over:

"Listen, Balmy, this is my stop. Here is a bottle of anti-gravity fuel I hid from you. It won't take you to Mars, but it will take you to Hollywood."

"Why Hollywood?"

"Because it's the only place where a man with green fur claws and a mouth on top of his skull won't stand out in a crowd. Tell them you're a standin for Boris Karloff. But don't say you are from Mars. They'll laugh at you.

Balmy's forelorn voice drifted down in me as the flying saucer spun westward:

"I'll look up Orson Welles. He'll recognize me."

And from here on in I'am riding nothing but file-mile-an-hour water wagons. They aren't driven by green guys from Mars.

The elements of the whole story are strongly ridiculous, including the huge hat-shaped spaceship and the look of the gigantic one-eyed Martian. They sound like a sort of extremization of the sighting news published by the press. That news reported much more mundane objects and lights in the sky, described or thought of as technological devices. They came with few details yet quite compatible (and acceptable) with the scientific breakthrough of that time or the foreseen near future. Something like that also happened during the 1897 airship wave and the many hoaxes involving encounters with completely human-like pilots, except for a few episodes involving odd "creatures from Mars."

Boyle's extremization was likely targeted at debunking the saucer craze, using elements seemingly taken from the sci-fi pulps that were considered rubbish by a large part of the population. Because of its substantial presence in popular culture, Mars was used as the most obvious home of the spaceman (who was hunting for Orson Welles too, which was related to Mars because of his 1938 radio hoax), confirming the presence of the much-debated water-filled canals.

Other yarn features are reminiscent of the later contactee stories, including the exotic anti-gravity propulsion, the trip aboard the saucer, and even the chance to pilot it. Boyle didn't invent anything new. He probably just took inspiration from the ultra-popular sci-fi comics and the less dominant but well-known sci-fi pulp stories, mixing them with current news (for example, the recurring extreme speed of 1,200 mph associated with the saucers). He just helped some concepts to reach a larger part of the population: the contactees of the 1950s just exploited and expanded those extraordinary concepts to offer fantastic stories with a widespread background.

A few other journalists used the original Boyle's yarn to publish similar stories in local papers, exploiting some of its elements. The Boyle story was reprinted or mentioned in some newspapers worldwide. For example, the Australian newspaper *The Argus* on July 10 wrote (about the satirical stories related to saucers):

> *One story concerns an alleged conversation that a reporter had in a saloon bar with a man from Mars, who took him for a flight on an Atom-powered dive, and brought him back to earth only after he had impressed upon him that he had to catch his edition.*

Another newspaper[20] reported that a subscriber called the *Herald-Dispatch,* a daily published in Virginia, and anxiously inquired if it was confirmed that Hal Boyle was the prisoner of the green-haired O'Rune from Mars aboard a flying saucer.

The US press published other amusing fictional stories penned by journalists during the 1947 wave, not counting the many photomontages featuring dishes or coffee saucers superimposed on city landscapes. People heard about the celestial visitors but had no chance (if not very rare and fuzzy pictures) to see them in the papers, so reporters helped them with a local setting and a lot of humor.

Sees a Little Man

By the Associated Press

At Janesville police were somewhat skeptical of a telephoned report shortly after midnight by a man who said he saw flying discs—just after he stepped out of a tavern.

Meanwhile, in Detroit police were told by an unidentified observer that he not only saw some discs, but "a little man was sitting on the first one, steering."

Monroe Evening Times July 7, 1947

'Little Man Steering'

Some of those stories heavily teased the saucers and the people who saw them, telling of "saucer editors" desperately watching the skies in search of those flying contraptions. Others were more fictional, involving weird encounters with the saucer pilots. They were usually introduced as unlikely rumors of possibly actual facts, just like what happened during the American airship scare of 1896-97, though in lower numbers. For example, concise news from an *Associated Press* dispatch claimed an unidentified observer would have told the Detroit police that he saw some discs and a little man was sitting on the first one, steering[21]. The story was usually published in a box on the front page of some local newspapers.

According to a paper[22] dated July 7, a woman called their office to tell that a 70-year-old relative had seen an object "shot by her window" at about 11:30 pm on June 19, 1947, even before Arnold's sighting. The object was "a little bigger than the moon, " and a slim figure was inside, dressed in what looked like a "Navy uniform."

---

[20] Kingsport News July 9, 1947

[21] Green Bay Press Gazette, Monroe Evening Times, Ironwood Daily Globe, The Rhinelander Daily News, The Wisconsin Daily Tribune July 7, 1947; Eau Claire Leader July 8, 1947

[22] Worcester Daily Telegram July 7, 1947

According to Bloecher[23] , residents of the Center and J Street neighborhood in Tacoma, Washington, claimed to have seen some objects, some of which landed on nearby roofs. Witnesses saw several "little people" who obviously disappeared upon the arrival of newsmen[24]. This story sounds like one of the many tall tales circulated in the American press in July 1947, exploited by scammers to have fun (or get some personal advantage) and by journalists to publish something more exciting and other than the "usual" tales of flying saucers.

In the 2005 updated online version[25] of Bloecher's survey about the 1947 wave, there is a reference to an article that supposedly appeared in the Pendleton *East Oregonian,* "following the publicity was given to Arnold's report." On June 24th, the same afternoon that Kenneth Arnold had his sighting on the western flank of Mount Rainier, an unidentified Pendleton, Oregon, man was driving along a rural road outside of Pendleton when he saw a large disc-shaped object hovering six feet over a nearby field. He could see "two short figures wearing green suits and white helmets" standing under the object. The figures "suddenly vanished," and the thing then "shot towards the Columbia River, made a big circle," and then disappeared toward the mountains.

Man sticks to his report

Stories of UFOs started in Pendleton 40 years ago

East Oregonian June 24, 1987

Unfortunately, no article of such a kind has been found in the *East Oregonian* issues published between late June and late July 1947. The description of the encounter and the saucer "pilots" was kind of an anomaly if compared to the 1947 cases and much more like a classic landing case with occupants from the 1950s. At first, it was thought the story was mistakenly dated to 1947.

23 Bloecher, Ted (1967) Report on the UFO Wave of 1947

24 Tacoma News Tribune July 8, 1947

25 http://nicap.org/waves/Wave47Rpt/ReportUFOWave1947_SectionI_Addendum.htm visited in August 2017.

After some research, the story's original source was found, and it appeared pretty different.
It was an *East Oregonian* article published on the 40th anniversary of the first flying saucer sighting. In 1987, Bill Schuening, an Oregon farmer, told a reporter to have seen a saucer-like object suspended five or six feet off the ground, 25 miles north of Pendleton[26]. He saw it the same day of Arnold's sighting, but he told about it once that story was published in the local newspaper, *The East Oregonian*.

At a certain point in the 1987 article, he said that the "shiny, silver objects were perfectly spherical, while Arnold reported the objects as more crescent-shaped." This sounds like a sort of contradiction against what was reported earlier in the article and what he claimed some lines later:

> *There were two little guys in green suits with white helmets standing right underneath it. They were no bigger than this (- holding his hands at waist level -). It didn't scare me at all.*

Schuening said he was too amazed to be frightened. The craft was completely silver, with no seams or doors. He watched the helmeted creatures for a few seconds and then

> *they were gone. How they got in (the craft) I'll never know. Suddenly they were just gone.*

A few seconds later, the object zipped away toward the river, made a big circle, and headed over the mountains. The sighting lasted nearly one minute.

We do not know how the reporter found the man. The story looks like a false memory or something like that, to say the least. Just like many present memories of fantastic close encounters placed in a distant past, next to the beginning of the flying saucer saga or in the golden age of the nut and bolts saucers of the 1950s, the Schuening story came up 40 years later.

It is likely his alleged memory was a recollection of stories and images coming from different sources he got from the pop culture of the previous decades. The vague memory of an unusual observation in 1947 and the 40th anniversary covered by the local newspapers could have made the man aware of an extraordinary experience, making it even more important than the classic Arnold sighting. It was an excellent way to feel like a local "star."

---

26 East Oregonian June 24, 1987

Schuening reported a sighting in late June 1947, but it was completely different. The man reported a formation of objects flying very high in the sky, so much so that he could not determine their shape, but he said they were similar to those Kenneth Arnold saw the same day. They were traveling at an unusual rate of speed and weaving in and out of formation[27].

In the few stories humorously involving close encounters of the third kind with the saucers, the pilots were usually described as "little men" (Boyle's yarn was an exception since it involved a giant green Martian). Their size was the main morphological diversity, making them exotic and funny: it was a great feature to portray out-of-this-world beings capable of pushing the saucer stories to the realm of ridicule.

Another seemingly close encounter of the third kind, most likely a joke, was briefly reported by a Nashville newspaper[28]. One man would have written the editor of *The Nashville Tennessean* a long letter describing his encounter with a couple of "Men from Mars" on a nearby flying field. The man claimed that these strange little men, "all heads and arms and legs, glowing like fireflies," landed and descended from a flying saucer as he drove along a highway. The man and the "Men from Mars" exchanged greetings in sign language, and then the saucer finally took off in a cloud of smoke. The ending part of the article was about a funny phone from a tipster operating a rooming house: he asked for a photographer to take a picture of "some real flying saucers." He told about a couple at first-floor front:

> Meanwhile, as newspaper office telephone calls on this latest form of mid-summer madness multiply, it's obvious that the subject is getting a grip on people.
>
> One man, apparently perfectly sane and sober, wrote the editor of The Nashville Tennessean a long, interesting letter about his brush with a couple of Men from Mars on a nearby flying field.
>
> These strange little men, "all heads and arms and legs, glowing like fireflies," landed and alighted from a flying saucer as he drove along a highway, the man wrote.
>
> The man from Nashville and the Men from Mars exchanged greetings (in sign language) and the sau[illegible] finally took off in a cloud of [illegible] so the letter says.

The Nashville Tennessean July 9, 1947

> *They'are throwing their own china ... and I really don't care, so long as they pick up the pieces.*

An additional funny story, published on the front page in a short article titled *CIRCLE-SILLY: SAILOR SEES A SOCIABLE SAUCERITE*, involved the likely tall tale of an encounter with a saucer little man.

> *Here is the disc yarn to end all saucer stories in a disc-dizzy nation. A merchant seaman who swore he never touched a drop, telephoned The Houston Post and said*

---

27 Klamath Falls Herald-News June 30, 1947

28 The Nashville Tennessean July 9, 1947. It seems it was published verbatim also by the Memphis Commercial Appeal, same day.

> *a big silver disc landed in front of him while he was walking on Route 149 in Acres Home addition. A little man, two feet tall and with a head the size of a basket ball, climbed out of the disc and shook hands with him, the seaman said, then climbed back in and whirled away into the blue. 'Did he look like a man from Mars?' the reporter asked. 'I dunno,' the seaman replied. 'I never saw a man from Mars.'*[29]

No. 553.

'Flying Saucer' Pilot Tells Record Reporter Americans Are Immature And Undemocratic

BY DEWITT E. CARROLL
Record Staff Writer

Now it can be told. The mysterious flying discs that have the entire country in an uproar are space ships from Mars. I know. Last night, I became the first—and last—inhabitant of this earth to interview an occupant of the saucer-shaped speedsters.

Groping my way home through an intense ground fog, after spending an hour or so with a sick friend, I stumbled over one of the discs at Walker Avenue and Tate Street. It was a silverish gray in color, as best I could see through the fog, and shaped something like two saucers fastened together. The disc was six feet in diameter and two feet thick at the center, tapering to a sharp rim.

As my shins cracked on the edge of the thing, a small manhole popped open in the center of the disc and a little man jumped out. After a brief wonderment as to who was blocking traffic and who should look where he was going, I sat down beside the little man and began the strangest conversation of my life.

"What in blazes?" I said to myself. And before I could give throat to my question, the little man had answered in my own thoughts. "We are from the Martian Department of Interplanetary Trade," he said. "Don't look so startled—we Martians have been conversing by telepathy so long we have no vocal cords."

The little Martian was pretty bright. It turned out that he had studied nuclear fission in kindergarten, and taken up more difficult subjects in the first grade. He was one of a dozen explorers sent to the earth to report on possibilities of opening interplanet trade routes. As we swapped thoughts, a buzzer sounded, and the Martian reached inside the disc. He plugged a couple of shiny black tubes into his ears and began talking—pardon me, thinking—with his home base.

The conversation was perfectly audible.

"Any report?" came a distant voice. "Roger," replied my companion. "Go ahead," came the terse answer, "and I hope you have better news than Squadron K. Stalin had them shot as spies."

"Not much better," returned the little Martian, heaving a small sigh. "This country is one tremendous contradiction. It has vast natural and productive resources, but in two years after its last war it hasn't begun to satisfy the demand for consumer goods. It claims to be a democracy, but one man can paralyze every major industry in the country whenever he wants to. Yeah, some guy with big, black antennae over his eyes.

"And another thing: any pressure group with enough power can block progressive legislation, or abolish restrictive regulations that keep them from making a potful of money . . . money . . . m-o-n-e-y. Look it up in the dictionary. . . . I think it's some ancient god . . . everybody down here worships it."

While the Martian back at his base searched the dictionary, the little fellow explained that ultra-sensitive thought receivers enabled him to read the mass mind while his space disc skimmed over the countryside, throttled down to 1,200 miles an hour.

Could But Won't

"Americans are capable of producing food, housing and automobiles . . . automobiles . . . those things we studied about in ancient history. They could, but they won't do it. Seems some of them are keeping supplies short so they can get more money for what they sell.

"The people are too busy trying to grab what they can, while they can get it. They apparently don't give a whoop what happens to their fellow citizens. Strictly a case of 14-karat greed. It's revolting. Most of them say they don't like it, but they haven't done anything to correct the situation.

"Until the Americans become more mature, I'd advise you to forget about this place. You can't rely on production, and our agents couldn't possibly find a place to live until 1979. The Americans think the housing shortage ought to ease up by then, if you want to send another expedition back here. . . . Okay, I'll take off right now."

Stung by the picture this explorer from Mars had painted of the land of the free and the home of the overcharged, I defended my country.

"Our housing situation isn't so bad," I told him. "Why, it only took me a year and a half to get an apartment. I could buy a $4,000 house for $10,000, one that was built in 1929. As for automobiles, I could get a $1,300 car with just 100 miles on it for $2,500 and a gallon of my life's blood."

The little Martian cut me short. "So-long, chump!" he thought as he scrambled back into his space ship. There was a soft, whirring sound. The disc skimmed up Walker Avenue at 1,200 miles an hour, looping the Woman's College overpass three times in exuberance before the Martian opened the throttle and sped homeward.

Greensboro Record July 8, 1947

Not a "real" (!) close encounter but equally fascinating was a pretty ironic story published by Dewitt E. Carroll, a reporter for the *Greensboro Record*, at the bottom of the front page of the issue dated July 8.

The article was basically focused on the rhetorical expedience of an interview with a Martian coming to Earth just to deliver a series of comments and criticism of the time's political, social, and economic situation. Such an approach was quite frequent before the Second World War and especially during the years of the so-called "Mars mania," but there were a few examples in that same year, 1947, too. The Martian represented wisdom and higher knowledge perfectly, so his claims looked very reputable.

Carroll merged the rhetorical figure of the "old" Martian with the "new" flying saucers, so the Martian arrived at Earth on board one of those mysterious crafts.

---

29 Houston Post July 9, 1947

The description of the early encounter provided by the reporter is strikingly similar to the claims of many witnesses of classic landing cases with occupants. The rest is the joke of his talk with the telepathic Martian, blatantly ridiculous yet somehow a precursor of the later contactee claims from the 1950s.

> *"It was a silverfish gray in color, as best I could see through the fog, and shaped something like two saucers fastened together. The disc was six feet in diameter and two feet thick at the center, tapering to a sharp rim."*
> *"... a small manhole popped open in the center of the disc and a little man jumped out. After a brief wonderment as to who should look where he was going, I sat down beside the little man and began the strangest conversation of my life."*
> *"The little Martian cut me short. 'So-long-chump!' he thought as he scrambled back into his space ship. There was a soft, whirring sound. The disk skimmed up Walker Avenue at 1,200 miles per hour, looping the Woman's College overpass three times in exuberance before the Martian opened the throttle and sped homeward."*

Here's Flying Saucer To End All Flying Saucers

HERE'S FLYING SAUCER as envisioned by artist after hearing latest "eyewitness" reports. This saucer has everything but the cup and a man from Mars in the cockpit. (International)

The Evening Independent July 8, 1947

The small size of the spaceship was a sort of constant in the mass of the 1947 sightings[30] and an element justifying the proportional size of the exotic little men piloting the saucers according to the fantasy of jokers and some common people. The "two saucers fastened together" description is similar to other stories published then and predates one of the most classic iconic images of the flying saucers. Moreover, the 1,200 mph speed was another constant in "serious" articles and jokes like that. That astonishing speed originally reported by Arnold was one of the key elements of the strangeness of those aerial contraptions, the proof of a technological wonder that contributed massively to making the saucers something extraordinary. That speed led many people to think the saucers (if real) were really something beyond our known capabilities: a secret weapon was the first choice, a spaceship from Mars the second one.

---

30 Most sightings, where a size estimation was available, reported small or even petite sizes for the saucers. The "discovery" of many faked saucers (crashed in streets or courtyards) contributed to this trend since they were small crude models assembled by pranksters using various poor gadgets.

According to a local newspaper[31], an unidentified guy from Abilene, employed as a dishwasher in a local cafe, sent a letter to their office. The letter was definitely joking and was used to close an article dealing pretty skeptically with the saucers. The letter in part read:

> *I had been all day washing dishes and was pretty well dished when I left for home. Arriving there I fortified myself with several bottles of cold beer. Feeling that I needed some more I spiked four more bottles with Vodka. To cool off I sat on the back porch and looking into the sky immediately began to see saucers. "On looking closely I could see little people peeking over the rims of the cups (it was saucers mind you). Each little men had a long flowing beard and as they passed each man waved a bottle of Vodka at me. Then came some more saucers with little witches on brooms herding them. I thought I put a little too much Vodka in the beer, but after reading the Reporter News am convinced that I really saw all this."*

On July 11, a Michigan newspaper[32] printed a fiction story signed by columnist Clint Dunathan. It was another funny abduction-like yarn clearly aimed at ridiculing the saucer craze. It is of great interest because it introduces a few motifs very similar to the most classic close encounters and contactee claims of the 1950s. However, they seem to be taken straight from a pulp science-fiction novel, and the description of the "pilot" is blatantly teasing. The shape and size of the spaceship (a dish with a raised cockpit in the middle) was a model that became the paradigm of the flying saucer in the popular imagination just very few years later. It had already been used in describing other 1947 tales, and some newspapers had published similar artworks during the wave before that story.

Here it is the Dunathan's story.

> *GOOD MORNING! By the Bugler*
> *By Clint Dunathan*
>
> *LIFE IN A SAUCER. Although we have not been pledged to secrecy in our knowledge of the "flying disk" or "flying saucer", we feel some hesitation in revealing that for a short time last Sunday afternoon we had a brief ride in one of them. The circumstances surrounding that experience are unbelievable. While pickining near Fayette that afternoon we had wandered into a nearby field where wild*

---

31 Abilene Reporter News July 9, 1947

32 The Escanaba Daily Press July 11, 1947

strawberries grew. We had a paper cup half-filled with the berries when we heard a strange wailing, unearthly as the sound made on a musical saw or a singing radio commercial. The sound came from behind a clump of screening cedars and before you could say "flying saucer" a figure pushed through the cedars and stood revealed in the bright sunlight.

JUSTUS PLUVIOUS – The legs and feet of the figure – all four of them – were encased in what appeared to be cellophane. The body resembled that of a man except there was no head or arms, and the unwinking eye, located in the umbilicus, was the size and color of a cold boiled potato without gravy. Where the head should have been there was only a mass of blue spaghetti-like tendrils that waved in the wind. One of the feet, marked "Western Hemisphere," raised itself off the ground and a high-pitched sing-song voice said:

"Hi Bud. Come with me, for the carriage awaits without."

"Without what." we asked.

"Don't be funny," said the voice peevishly. "You're going for a ride." As it spoke an atomic ray gun popped out of its spaghetti and aimed at us "Come." The gun waved threateningly. The figure turned and began to walk around the cedars and we followed because the gun was still pointed at us. When the feet were lifted to step over a log we saw where the voice came from. There was a mouth in the bottom of each foot. And on the back of the figure in raised letters that flashed like a neon sign over a tavern were the words "Justus Pluvious."

The Escanaba Daily Press July 11, 1947

THE INVISIBLE INFRA -- Still clutching the paper cup and the strawberries we followed hesitantly. There on the other side of the cedars was a flat, dish-like silvery like colored contraption about 20 feet in diameter with a center area raised about three feet. It resembled a saucer with half an egg shell in the middle. "A flying saucer!" we exclaimed. We turned to run, but there was a sudden dull thud, the sound of a falling body and a feeling as fi if we were whirling through space.

ATOMIC MUTATIONS -- Regaining consciousness we found ourselves reclining on a plastic-like yet soft floor that was the bottom of the "flying saucer." Near us, with all four feet working the controls, was Justus Pluvious. Below, through the floor, could be seen the rapidly changing map-work of the earth over which we skimmed at terrific speed. "Did anyone ever tell you that you looked like your mother had been frightened by a comic book?" we asked idly. The foot marked "Western Hemisphere" relaxed on the controls. "So you're awake, Mayor Coon." Justis chuckled from all four feet and his boiled potato eye winked "When we reach the Jupiterian master technician, you can repeat that crack. He has more atomic transmutations than I have. "I'm not Mayor Coon." "What! Who are you, then." "One of the Rack Coons from an old Southern family," quipped. We asked him why he wanted a mayor, and Justus explained that he and other atomic transmutes from Jupiter had been sent out on a scouting expedition to Earth to gather data for its plastic surgeons. The surgeons were planning a series of mass operation on the Jupiterian transmutes to make them more beautiful and in the likeness of earthlings. They particularly wanted models who were noted in public life, including mayors, presidents, deputy sheriffs and car salesmen. We said we worked for a newspaper. By this time we were skimming over California at an extremely high altitude, and we mumbled something about models such a Gregory Peck and Dorothy Lamour. Justis asked if they were deputy sheriffs and we said no, movie stars. "Never heard of them." he said shortly, "and the master technician won't want you, either."

STRAWBERRY RASH-- The "flying saucer" whirled suddenly in its course and headed back towards Michigan. Justus grew hungry and with one foot nibbled at a concentrated energy pill that flashed different colors. Red was meat flavor, green was celery or string beans, pink was strawberry ice cream. "Strawberry is my favorite," he said. "Have a real strawberry." we said, holding out the paper cup. "Well, just one or two." he said "I always get a rash." he explained. He took one in his toes curled them under and nibbled daintily. " Hm, very good. He ate all of them. When we were over Keokuk - or maybe it was Des Moines – Justus suddenly started to change color and groan. He had the most beautiful case of strawberry rash we had ever seen. He continued to groan and writhe in agony until we touched the ground at Fayette, where he ordered us out. Then with his foot he turned a dial marked "Atomic Disintegration," and he and the "flying saucer" disappeared in a flash. All that was left at the spot was a short piece of spaghetti and a cold boiled potato and those might have been thrown away by a picnic party.

Four days later[33], Dunathan wrote his apologies to a lady who telephoned the same day of the publication of his column to ask whether it was truth or fiction. He confirmed it was pure fiction and, so far as he knew, the flying saucers were not operated by four-footed Jupiterians. But he didn't want to disappoint the reader completely:

---

33 The Escanaba Daily Press July 15, 1947

... our guess is as good as anyone's until somebody captures a "flying saucer" and finds out otherwise.

Boyle's Flight Over Sioux Falls?

After three days of reading story after story about flying saucers, Wilmer Simmons, telegraph editor of The Argus-Leader, who is normally a quiet, sane individual, went berserk. He grabbed his camera and ran out of the building shrieking at the top of his voice.

He rushed to the East Tenth street viaduct with intentions of ending it all. Just then he looked up in the sky. There it was—a flying saucer! He couldn't believe it. But he snapped this picture to prove it.

He felt better after that. He returned to work. Now, people think he is just as sane as ever.

The Daily Argus Leader July 9, 1947

Several American newspapers published amusing photo montages of plates or dishes flying over urban landscapes. This was an ironic way to depict those strange contraptions reported by many people and mock them, as well as the entire story.

This Sioux Falls (South Dakota) newspaper published the second part of Boyle's story on the front page, including a nice photo montage. It was an excellent way to illustrate the article published concurrently by hundreds of dailies across the United States with a local flavor.

Here they are! Early crashes of flying saucers: a short visual history

Just after Independence Day of 1947, flying saucers became the top favorite argument of most people in the US, and the newspapers (and the radio as well) kept offering an outstanding wealth of information for about one week. Although most people claimed to be skeptical about those gadgets reported in the American skies, a vast majority of them were curious at least and eager to see one of them.

Moreover, the common idea was that whether those contraptions really flew in large numbers all over the States, they had to crash sooner or later. People were waiting for the ultimate chance to see a flying saucer and finally understand what it was. Some journalists hoped the same in their comment columns. In a few sporadic cases, this seemed to happen. For example, an *Associated Press* dispatch quoted by a few newspapers[34] reported that three hunters claimed to have seen scores of shining objects whirling over Wild Horse Park, a remote area in Colorado. Reaching the spot where the objects appeared to have plunged to the ground, they found flat plates of burned-out matter, ranging in size from a saucer to a soup plate and golden brown. They said they were on an extended hunting expedition, unaware of the excitement stirred up by the reports of flying discs, and they did not return with any of their finds.

At the end of the very first week of the saucer era, a "shining disc" was found on the ground. One Troy Pendergrass said he chased a flying disc on June 29 in Ash Canyon, New Mexico:

> *"it looked bright as a mirror"*

and then, with some friends, he found it on the ground. It was just a five-by-eight-inch piece of tinfoil, slightly heavier than that used for gum wrappers, and was very crinkled. It looked like it had been wrapped around a circular object, partially burned and melted[35]. Two even too enthusiastic guys in Portland found another funny contraption in early July. Everything was good for a "disc": it was just a 3x2 foot piece of white paper of cheap quality, slightly yellowed around the edges. It fluttered down from an estimated altitude of 4,000 feet to land on a golf course. Then it was turned over to *The Oregonian* newspaper for "scientific examination."[36]

---

[34] Walla Walla Union Bulletin, The Tipton Daily Tribune, The McKinney Daily Courier-Gazette July 9,1947

[35] The Gallup Independent, Abilene Reporter News, The Oregon Statesman, Dallas Morning News, The Paris News July 1, 1947

[36] The Oregonian July 5, 1947

The Des Moines Regitser July 6, 1947

For some of those people, finding anything a bit stranger than usual was enough to satisfy their curiosity. Weather balloons or parts of them began to be reported in the press on July 5[37]. They predated the Roswell "crash" story, showing similar descriptions.

The husband of Mrs. Sherman Campbell from Circleville, Ohio, found a six-pointed, tinfoil-covered star-like object on their farm, about 50 inches high and 48 inches large. A balloon was attached to the star. Several newspapers published a couple of different photos of Mrs. Sherman holding the "flying disc" until July 9[38], peaking on July 7. Several other cases of grounded balloons (or parts of them) followed in the next days and weeks, but they were local episodes that usually never left the pages of local newspapers.

The Daily Reporter 7 July 1947

Other people exploited the saucer craze to make fun of some specific persons or the neighbors. Saucers were a robust and fresh topic, and everybody was ready to consider it and give it a lot of coverage. Something similar had already happened in other situations in the past, including the relevant airship wave that happened in the US between November 1896 and April 1897 (the 1947 newspapers sometimes quoted it, reporting the memories of a few old persons who still recalled those events). In that 50-year-old wave, the "yellow journalism" of the time contributed to several hoaxes.

---

37 The Circleville Herald July 5, 1947; Columbus Daily Dispatch, The Des Moines Register July 6, 1947

38 Richmond Palladium, The Bismarck Tribune, Casper Star Tribune July 9, 1947

After publishing news about rewards that industrialists, associations, and department stores promised for a "real" flying saucer, several crashed discs appeared in courtyards or gardens throughout the United States. There were several tens of episodes of such a kind[39]. Some gained nationwide notoriety, and a few even triggered an investigation by the FBI or the Army. After over 75 years, it is tough to understand how it was even possible to consider those silly contraptions as something "strange." They were crude or extremely crude homemade gadgets that even the most naive guy could not consider seriously today. But in 1947, although usually regarded as laughable, they were "accepted" and often introduced by the newspapers as a funny solution for those flying things reported in the sky. Nobody knew what the saucers were, so everything was possible, and they were a good chance to talk about them with something at hand.

Spokane Daily Chronicle 14 July 1947

As told before, those crashed saucers were also thought of as a way to solve the mystery and cash in the high rewards naively promised all around the country (from $1,000 to $8,000, which means something about between $14,000 and $111,000 at today's values). One reward seems to have been paid in one case, at least.

On July 13, the Spokane Athletic Round Table would have paid $1,000 for a "reasonable facsimile"[40] of a disc. Four boys at the Washington State children's home heard an explosion and rushed out to find a highly burnished disk lying in scorched grass or the trees near the home, according to a local newspaper publishing a photograph on its front page[41].

---

39 American UFO student Kenny Young published online a *CHRONOLOGICAL DATABASE OF 1947 FLYING SAUCER CRASHES* at http://kenny.anomalyresponse.org/47index.html The list is a good reference work but still to be completed with other several entries.

40 Walla Walla Union Bulletin July 15, 1947

41 Spokane Daily Chronicle July 14, 1947

Likely, it was just a funny way to exploit the news of the day to introduce a previously scheduled donation. The Round Table frequently made gifts to small schools and orphanages for sports programs, and the club's members seemed to know just where to go to examine the disk. Later, they announced that the money had to go toward constructing a new gymnasium for the orphan children.

The desire to get their own name in the local newspaper and have a "real saucer" to show proudly to their friends were equally strong motivations to spend time creating a gadget. People seemed to be making fun of finding and discussing those "crashed saucers." Generally speaking, it was a sort of popular attraction, a cheap amusement not necessarily related to the idea of a secret weapon or another exotic source. However, technology was the driving concept of the crude models prepared by the pranksters.

This chapter puts together a short visual history of some of those little flying saucers that amused many American readers during the summer of 1947, extensively using rare photographs usually published by obscure local American newspapers. I will deal with the events reported with some photographic evidence only, namely a minority of all the retrieval cases published by the press during the summer of that year.

The Philadelphia Enquirer July 8, 1947

CRASH-LANDED SAUCERS

One of the earliest findings of crashed discs got colossal press coverage all over the United States, even with pictures on the front pages, and it was reported by some foreign papers, too.

It was that funny and improbable contraption to be likely used as a prototype for the nonsense of all the saucer stories that were becoming overwhelming in those days. Press and radio used it for ironic comments and gags (for example, using joking titles like "He saw a saw"), sometimes delivering conflicting news.

Life July 21, 1947

A Catholic priest, Joseph Brasky of St. Joseph Church at Grafton, Wisconsin, said he heard a whizzing noise the morning of July 6. He heard a "bang!" like a firecracker a second later. Brasky stepped outside and found a sheet metal disc on the church lawn. It was about 18 (or 15) inches in diameter, resembling a circular saw blade with a jagged edge and saw teeth. Although the grass was still wet from the night rain, the object was still warm (as reported by a *United Press* dispatch, but according to other reports, "it was too hot to handle"[42]), weighed about four or five pounds, and was about one eight of an inch thick.

It looked greasy and somewhat dirty. In the middle of the disc was a one and three-eighths-inch hole, and in the opening were "gadgets and some wires," while other sources refer to a peculiar wiring arrangement from the middle to the outside edge.

42 Milwaukee Journal Sentinel July 7,1947

Life July 21, 1947

To each end of the cluster of wires was attached what looked like a small condenser about three inches long and wrapped in still sticky black tape. Father Brasky said he had notified the FBI of his find[43]: supposedly, the object struck one of the church lighting rods because a glass ball had been knocked off it.

Friends of the priest knew he was the well-known author of the "Fish Tales" book: Father Charlie was sure that the disc was taken off Brasky's buzz-saw[44]. The FBI identified the disk as a circular saw, bearing the label of a mail order house and a marking reading "… Steel, high carbon100 percent steel" ("Approved, Dunlap," according to another source), noticed the first time by Father Brasky when he examined the object closely.

The Shreveport Times July 8, 1947

A "saucer" was found on the late afternoon of July 7 in Shreveport, Louisiana. The front page of a local newspaper[45] reported the episode, but it found space in many papers all over the States. Unlike other cases, a man claimed to have heard and seen the disc whirling through the air, and then he retrieved it from the middle of the street. This F.G. "Happy" Harston said it "came over a signboard adjacent to the lot" from a northerly direction.

---

43 Rocky Mountains News, Dayton Journal July 7,1947

44 The McHenry Plaindealer July 10,1947

45 The Shreveport Times July 8,1947

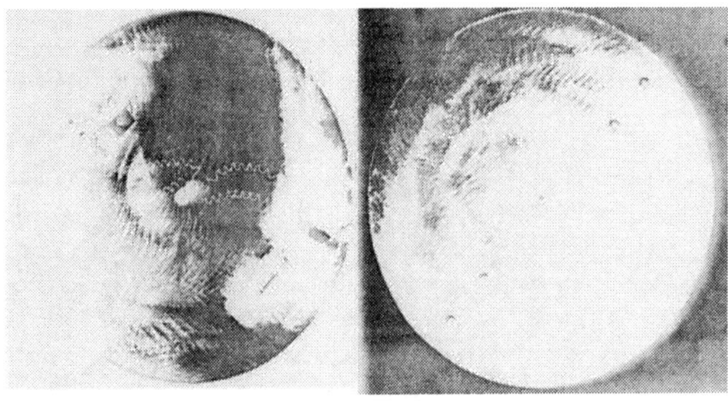

Foto nel rapporto FBI del July 23, 1947

It was flaming as it spun but was cold when he picked it up. The object was a 16-inch aluminum disc on which two tubular radio condensers were mounted, a fluorescent light "starter," and some copper wire. Probably someone hurled the disc after coating it with some inflammable substance and igniting it before launching. An FBI agent examined it, and the local police then turned it over to a military base.

The Cincinnati Times-Star July 8, 1947

An airplane wing tip was found on July 7 and immediately called a "flying saucer." Some employees of the night shift of the Southern's Railroad Ludlow coach yard, Kentucky, picked up a piece of metal wing from a dismantled plane, which had fallen from a carload of scrap. On the wing tip, they chalked "Half a flying saucer." The local police chief and newspaper journalists quickly exposed the practical joke[46].

Tucson Daily Citizen July 8, 1947

On July 8, the same day the Roswell story emerged in the American newspapers, an Arizona paper[47] published a photograph depicting two reporters examining the remnants of a "flying saucer" found at a ranch 12 miles south near the Nogales highway. It was just a "radiosonde modulator" sent aloft by weather balloons.

---

46 The Cincinnati Post, The Cincinnati Times-Star, The Kentucky Post July 8,1947

47 Tucson Daily Citizen July 8,1947

ELDON GOLDEN
. . . a real jockey (disc variety)

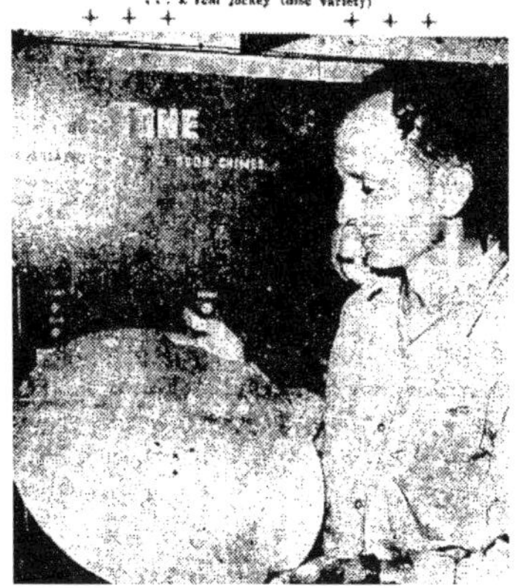

Amarillo Daily News July 9, 1947

The day after, in Amarillo, Texas, a young electrical contractor named W.J. Wisdom was riding along a highway with his wife. They saw a reflected flash of light from something near the highway and close to a radio tower. The man picked up the shiny object: it was an aluminum disc with three holes. Later, after publishing the story on its front page, a reporter and a local newspaper photographer went to the local KGNC radio station. He got confirmation that the object was just a radio recording disc.

The newspaper[48] joked about it, closing the article with

"… and that made electrical man Wisdom the first man in the nation to confirm his "disc" really was a disc."

Enticed by the $ 3,000 reward reported by many newspapers, some boys in Rochester, New York, brought discs to the police for investigations. They were immediately considered crude boy pranks. A 14-inch cardboard disc was found and photographed on a treetop.

Beaver Valley Times July 9, 1947

48 Amarillo Daily News July 9,1947

Beaver Valley Times July 9, 1947

It looked like a part of a hat box or some similar container. A 15-year-old girl found it, claiming to have heard it whizzing through the sky before landing[49].

A jokester attached two small balloons to an ordinary coffee cup and let it fly. It was then found in a gutter near Greentown, Ohio, where it crashed because one of the balloons broke [50].

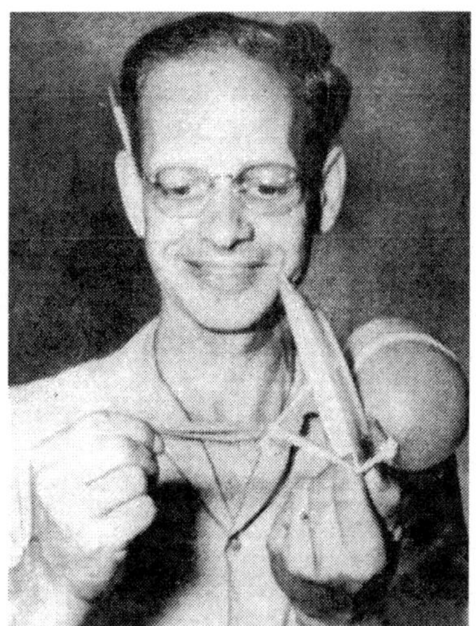

The Akron Beacon Journal July 9, 1947

Arizona Daily Star July 10, 1947

A much more complex gadget was put together by the employees of an Arizona company using the descriptions provided by the people claiming to

49 Beaver Valley Times July 9,1947

50 The Akron Beacon Journal July 9,1947

have seen the mysterious flying discs[51]. It was carried down a street on the afternoon of July 9 without arousing a single comment from pedestrians. The gadget was 24 inches in diameter, made from shiny aluminum, and loaded with a burned-out radar tube, coils, and other business-like parts.

Binghamton Press July 10, 1947

That same July 9, another "retrieval" took place in North Hollywood, California, immediately becoming one of the most popular episodes of the 1947 wave, covered by hundreds of newspapers, often on the front page. Many published pictures of the "disc," especially one depicting it on the desk of Fire Chief Wallace Newcomb, were later used by magazines, including a popular weekly in 1949[52].

Some firemen recovered a metal 30-inch disc-shaped object in a garden. According to an FBI report dated July 17, an unknown woman had called the local fire department, reporting that a disc had dropped in her garden, where it began to flame. A truck was sent there and put out the flaming object with the fire hose; then, it was taken to the fire station.

RECOVERY OF "FLYING DISC", NORTH HOLLYWOOD, CALIFORNIA, JULY 9, 1947

FBI pictures of the North Hollywood disc

---

51 Arizona Daily Star July 10,1947

52 Saturday Evening Post May 7, 1949

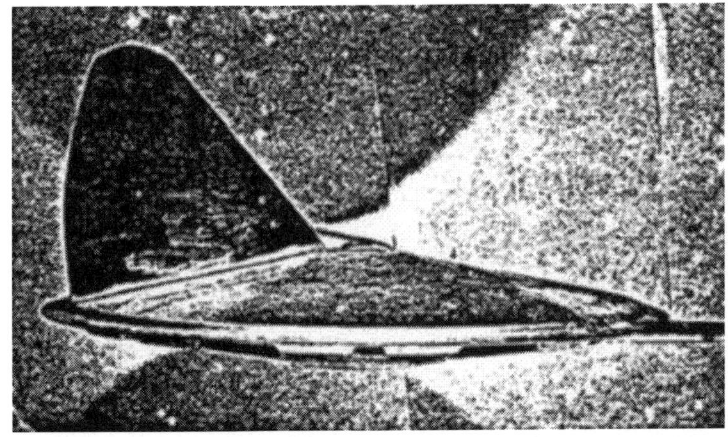

Another picture of the North Hollywood disc

Most newspapers reported Russell Long, a construction engineer, as the man who called the fire department to claim that a flashing and smoking disc had landed in his flower garden. The gadget was made of two convex steel discs fused at the outer edge and fastened in the center by a hollow cylindrical connection.

A vertical galvanized iron fin was screwed to the top of the disc, and a short length of pipe closed at one end ran from the outer circumference into the interior of the object. A radio tube was mounted in the center of the top side. It was a hoax[53], and many papers highlighted that it had happened just in Hollywood [54].

The Chicago Tribune July, 18

July 9 was the favorite day for pranksters, just following the top coverage of saucer news in the American press, fuelled by the announcements of generous rewards for those bringing a genuine flying disc. A Ralph S. Waterbury found a circular object in his yard at Arlington Heights, Illinois[55].

Wilmington Daily Press July 18, 1947

53 The same FBI document dated July 17 quoted someone (name blackened) reporting about a group of young high school students he met in a North Hollywood service station, where there was considerable talk about the disc found in the vicinity. He got a definite impression they either had themselves or knew of someone who had been working for the "past two weeks" making the disc.

54 Binghamton Press July 10,1947

55 The Chicago Tribune July 10,1947

Iowa City Press Citizen July 12, 1947

It was about 17 inches in diameter and had two insulators, two ceramic condensers, and a radio frequency choke affixed to it. The disk was just an old broadcast transcription record.

A picture depicting Mrs. Ruth Waterbury (possibly the man's wife) showing the disc next to her dog was published by some newspapers across the States, sometimes on the front page[56].

Other pranksters left a metallic disc in the hedge of the front yard of Mr. William Kindl's home in Iowa City, Iowa. It was composed of two aluminum cake pans sealed together at the rims with a type of gold solder. Inside was an array of electrical apparatus, including a gold-painted radio tube, a large cork, wires, and miscellaneous other gadgets.

The caption introducing the photo[57] of the man with the disc commented ironically about the "possible" Martian origin of the gadget:

> *If men from Mars flew to earth in the 'flying disc' above, they must have been pretty small, or possibly they were gremlins.*

Some people seemed ready to sell anything for a flying saucer or its remnants. Although the significant amount of money the rewards promised during the peak days of the wave was a distant mirage, they could get the personal gratification of having their names published in the local newspaper or even beyond.

The Waterloo Courier July 12, 1947

---

56 The Courier Gazette, The Daily Reporter July 15, 1947; The Kane Republican July 16,1947

57 Iowa City Press Citizen July 10,1947

The Bismarck Tribune July 12, 1947

Again, on July 9 in Iowa, Carl Larsen found a sort of burned fabric and what looked like carbon ash in a cornfield. For some unknown reason, such a substance was related to a flying disk.

A few pranksters wanted "to see what would happen" and test the gullibility of the people in their community.

An episode on July 11 in North Dakota was paradigmatic. Five men built a saucer during the night and placed it on the lawn of the Miller family in Woodworth, where it was found in the early morning. Hundreds of visitors flocked to the place on foot, by car, and in planes[58].

The Bismarck Tribune July 12, 1947

The men admitted the hoax, claiming they built the saucer from the bottom of a wash tub, a lampshade, some tubes, wiring from weather observing equipment, some strands of human hair, and miscellaneous electrical equipment. The object had been painted with a thick cover of silver paint and had a propeller that turned out to be the fan blades of an automobile heater, with the letters "X441" and "Delco Appliance Corporation" on its side[59].

58 The Bismarck Tribune July 12,1947

59 St. Cloud Times, Rapid City Journal July 11,1947

As in other cases of "crashed saucers," the military (and the FBI) was involved in understanding what was happening. They were likely overwhelmed by the gigantic amount of information reported by the press (and to a lesser, yet important, extent by the radio) influencing people and popular thinking in those weeks. They were worried about this and the possibility that foreign aircraft could be behind the sightings. Still, all that mess made them pretty confused and prone to investigate even blatant hoaxes, such as the unlikely discs found in yards and gardens. The fact that the military or the FBI used their time to follow (and later report) those and other ridiculous episodes was later exploited by diehard UFO believers to show that something should exist for real. Hearing of the Woodworth "saucer," Capt. G.W. McCoy, Army Air Forces liaison officer of the North Dakota wing of the Civil Air Patrol, called Army intelligence headquarters in Washington for instructions. McCoy was given orders to see that the object was "watched and closely guarded" and to have it brought to CAP headquarters in Fargo. He was also told to see that "as little publicity as possible" be given to the object[60]. The five men seemingly confessed their hoax just after McCoy's involvement[61].

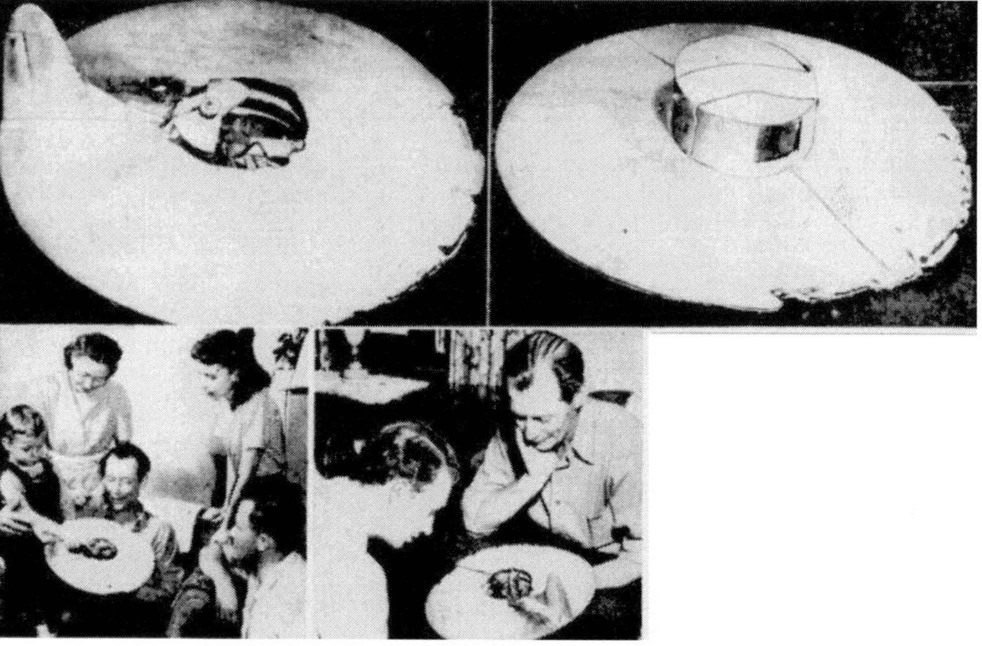

La Crosse Tribune July 11, 1947

60 The Argus Leader, Daily Illini July 12,1947

61 Palladium Item July 12,1947

La Crosse Tribune July 12, 1947

On July 10, another find took place in Black River Falls, Wisconsin[62] , and was reported by several newspapers across the United States. Sigurd Hanson, a city electrician, came across a saucer-shaped object in a field of the local fairgrounds. At that spot, a mark of about five to six feet(1.5 - 1.8 meters) was visible in the grass where the object skidded[63].

It was like two medium-sized soup bowls placed together, silver in color and reflecting light. It had a sort of motor, the size of a man's fist, set in the center and a two-inch propeller with two metal blades. The gadget also had a radio tube (a photo-electric cell with the letters "R.C.A.") and a four-inch vertical fin. Next to the latter, there was a scorched section: the caption of a photo depicting it suggested that

> *jet propulsion may have been used to launch the unusually constructed object.*

It was about 15.5 inches in diameter and weighed about 1.5 pounds. Lt. Frederick Frederickson, CAP squadron commander at Black River Falls, asked CAP authorities to inspect the mysterious disc. Then Col. Harry W. Schaefer, commanding officer of the Wisconsin Civil Air patrol[64], went to Black River Falls to examine the object and later reported his findings to the army officials.

La Crosse Tribune July 11, 1947

---

62 Green Bay Press Gazette, Marshfield News Herald, Monroe Evening Times, Racine Journal Times, Milwaukee State Journal July 11,1947; Eau Claire Leader, The Daily Tribune July 12,1947

63 La Crosse Tribune July 11,1947

64 A few days before, Schaefer had been quoted by many American newspapers about the planned patrolling of the skies in search of the flying discs.

He thought it was a hoax, but he wasn't sure. The local Chamber of Commerce locked the disk in a bank vault and refused to give it to Schaefer to bring to Milwaukee[65]. The Chamber of Commerce did much more. It displayed the disc at 20 cents (plus tax) per look, expecting "a thousand" persons on Sunday, July 13. Mr Hanson turned the disc over to the Chamber: it was placed in a glass case in the armory of their building, and two men were to guard it while on exhibit. The proceeds were to go to Hanson, who also expected "to collect the reward money offered for an explanation of the flying saucer mystery,"[66] namely the $ 1,000 reward offered by the World Inventor Congress in session those days at Hollywood, California. Hanson was already considering using that money to build a garage and porch at his house[67].

La Patrie July 12, 1947

The discs were found in Canada, too. A one Mrs. F. Brown from Toronto showed a round object (curiously having a sort of aperture in the rear, similar to later saucer imagery) with a copper tube on a side and a cardboard roller above[68].

The day after, another episode was reported from London, Ontario. A cylinder of the same size as a regular stovepipe was found on the evening of July 11 on the grass of Mrs. Alton Upthegrove's summer house. According to a Canadian newspaper[69], nobody knew where the object came from, but it would have been seen "land in a trail of light."

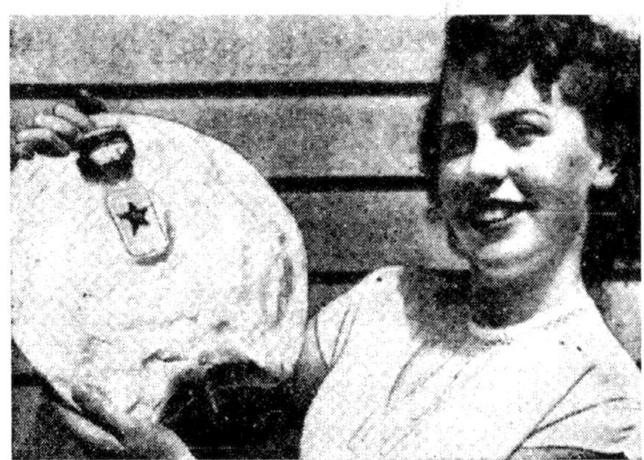

La Patrie July 11, 1947

65 Milwaukee State Journal July 12,1947

66 Eau Claire Leader, La Crosse Tribune July 13, 1947

67 La Crosse Tribune July 11,1947

68 La Patrie July 11,1947

69 La Patrie July 12,1947

The Minneapolis Star July 11, 1947

The Minneapolis Star July 11, 1947

Two more findings came from Minneapolis[70], back in the USA. Mr. Eugene Peterson was working in his garden when an object came hurtling over a nearby fence. After inspection, it was made of two tin plates, one of which was attached to a shaky propeller. Inside it were a Roman candle, a gasoline-soaked rag, and the top of a pepper can. Mr. E.H. Moehlenbrock, who operated a tree and plant nursery, found the remains of a disk in his tomato plants.

It had no means of propulsion and was made from two sheet metal cones joined together. It was empty and had three 18-inch "legs" (a sort of landing gear) on one side. The man thought it might have been a smokestack ventilator.

A certain Joseph Kemper found a large disc in a cornfield north of York, Pennsylvania, and brought it to the local police headquarters. It was made from aluminum, with the size of a large radio record. It had several tubes, condensers, resistors, and other paraphernalia soldered on, and some rubber tubing was attached. The object had some alleged Oriental characters painted over it in red[71].

---

70 The Minneapolis Star July 11,1947

71 The Gazette and Daily July 12,1947

The Gazette and Daily July 12, 1947

The abundance of technological add-ons, in this and other episodes alike, was likely a naive attempt of the pranksters to give a high-tech look to what was believed to be a sort of Buck Rogers stuff.

On July 11, another finding of a "flying disc" got extensive national notoriety, being published by hundreds of newspapers (also abroad), often on the front page[72]. A 30.5-inch object with a rugged metal dome on one side and a frosted plexiglass dome about 14 inches high[73] on the opposite side was found anchored in place by what appeared to be stove bolts at Twin Falls, Idaho. It was gold painted on one side and silver on the other, and it seemed to have been turned out by machine. Stamped into the metal near the disc's outer edge were the words "Inspected by TM."

Mrs. Fred Easterbrook found it after she "heard a crash" in a yard near her home around 2:30 (but the saucer had already been left there a few hours before ...).

LATE BULLETIN

Times-News

MAGIC VALLEY EDITION

Rift With Red Bloc Widening

Shades of Buck Rogers! This Is What Landed in Twin Falls

Attention Focuses On City as 'Disc' Is Found in Yard

11,000 Acres Burned In Fire at Minidoka

Ten Per Cent Drop in Meat Supplies Seen

Special Report Set On 'State-of-Nation'

Egypt Appeals For Ouster of Briton Troops

Two Hurt in Plane Crash Near Heglar

FLASHES of LIFE

Senate Boost In Funds for Land Agreed

Rails Plead for Higher Mail Pay

Elko Grass Fire Is Under Control

Water Pressure Improvement at Burley Planned

Unveiled Yesterdays Windows Draw Throngs of Spectators

No Trace in Film Taken by Boiseans

Wanted: An Old Stagecoach for Yesterdays Fete

Flight Promised At Legion Meet

Twin Falls Times News July 11, 1947

---

[72] The Miami News, Honolulu Star Bulletin, East Oregonian, Salt Lake Telegram, Twin Falls Times News July 11,1947

[73] Another source reported the whole contraption was approximately 12 inches thick from dome peak to dome peak.

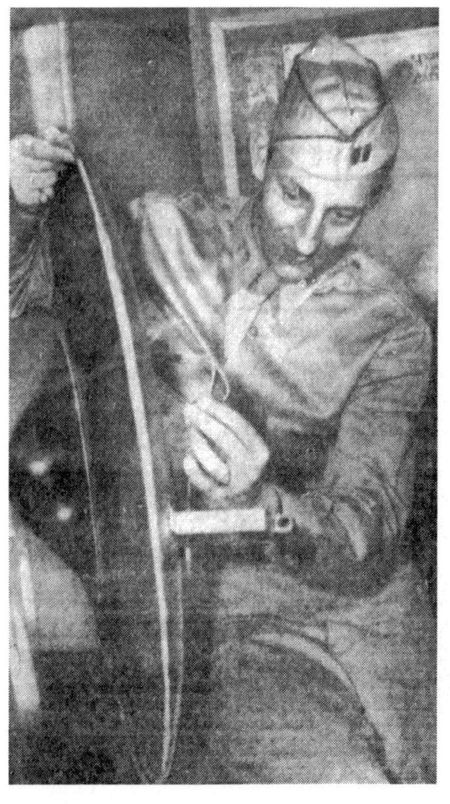

Lewiston Morning Tribune July 13, 1947

An FBI agent inspected the gadget and described it as similar to the "cymbals used by a drummer in a band, placed face to face," adding that he could see three radio tubes inside the plastic dome. The case was reported to the FBI office in Butte, Montana, and military intelligence at Ft. Douglas, Utah: army officers from the fort went to Twin Falls by plane and took the object to their base. They also confiscated all the pictures of the object; the only photos were those taken by local police[74].

The day after, four boys confessed to the hoax. According to an *Associated Press* dispatch, the boys created and planted in a yard "an object that looked to them, as well as to the army and civilian officers, just like a flying disc should look."

It seems that the concept of a (doubled) domed disc had been becoming quite dominant in the popular imagination; other sketches, artworks, and tales published by the papers in those weeks seem to confirm such a trend. The object was completed in two days, using parts of an old phonograph, burned-out radio tubes, and other discarded electrical parts[75].

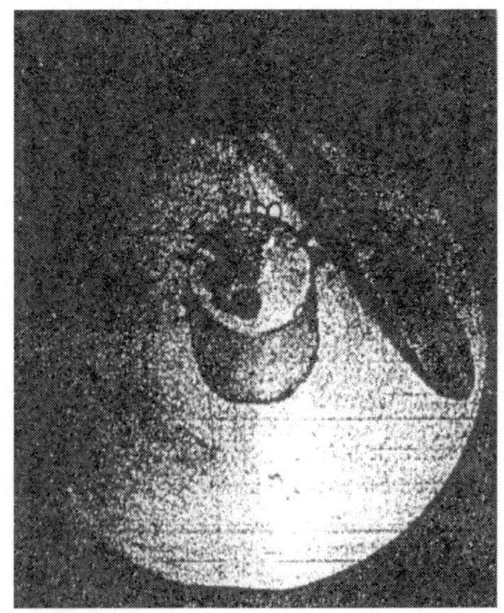

The Greely Daily Tribune July 12, 1947

74 Twin Falls Times News July 13, 1947

75 Asbury Park Press, Buffalo Courier Express, Chicago Tribune, Harrisburg Telegraph, Lewiston Morning Tribune July 12,1947

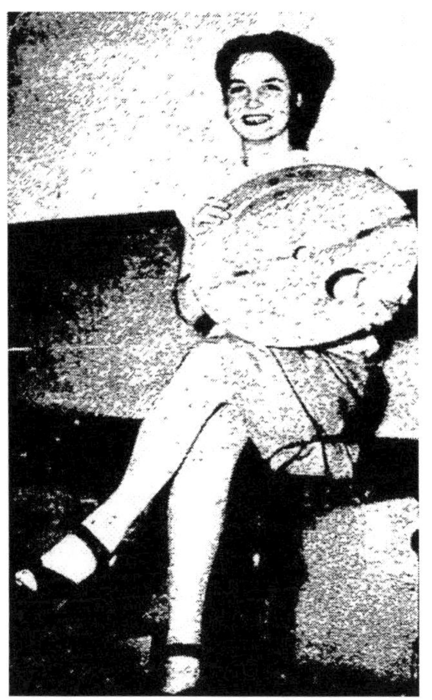

The Zanesville Times Recorder July 13, 1947

Another prank took place in Greely, Colorado. A boy claimed to have found a smoking disc made from a phonograph record, a couple of pieces of wire, a metal cover, a fusa, and some balsa wood for a propeller. The caption introducing the photo of the disc in the local weekly wisely read:

It probably is a fair replica of what some people expect the so-called flying disks to be.

The store owner exploited the story and the saucer craze, offering $10 for the best model of a flying disc[76].

On July 12, one of those baffling discs was seen landing with a crash near Zanesville, Ohio. A farmer driving his truck after 2:00 pm heard a strange whirring noise in the sky. Poking his head from the truck cab saw something falling from the sky and crashing a short distance in front of him. The farmer walked around the object once or twice before stepping up and throwing it in the back of his truck. When he reached Zanesville, he went to a service station for gas: he recounted his story to the attendants and left the disc there. The "saucer" was an 18-inch aluminum hubcap from a transport airplane that had fallen while the plane was flying over the area[77].

The Lowell Sun July 15, 1947

A little boy in Lowell, Massachusetts, found a quarter-inch-thick copper plate in a field. It was six three-eighth inches in diameter and had some printed letters and numbers. It was quickly revealed as the work of some joker when a local newspaper reporter went to the spot[78].

---

76 The Greely Daily Tribune July 12,1947

77 The Zanesville Times Recorder July 13, 1947

78 The Lowell Sun July 15, 1947

Yankton Press & Dakotan July 15, 1947

At Yankton, South Dakota, somebody left a disc on the lawn of a house on July 13. It was metallic and about 21 inches in diameter, on which some stuff had been mounted: used radio parts, a slender tube resembling a fly-spray container, a drap hanger ring, a network of wires leading nowhere in particular, and an upright metal rod appearing as the "antenna."

All this was painted green, and affixed to the assemblage were the figures 257 and a swastika, while on the lid were the figures 57018, all in ordinary decals. The whole thing appeared to be the lid of some large shipping container[79].

In the dead of the night on July 15, Mr. C.H. Hancock from Denton, Texas, heard a metallic sound: he thought two cars had clicked fenders. He went outside and found an object left by somebody in his front yard: pranksters had evidently struck it with a hammer. The disc had four spark plugs[80].

Denton record Chronicle July 16,1947

People kept reporting strange things on the ground that could be one of those mysterious flying contraptions reported by many people. It was also an excellent way to share a popular attraction and become part of the general excitement. Miss Jo Harris found a 7-inch large, flat, shiny metal disc stuck edgewise in a vegetable garden at Andalusia, Illinois.

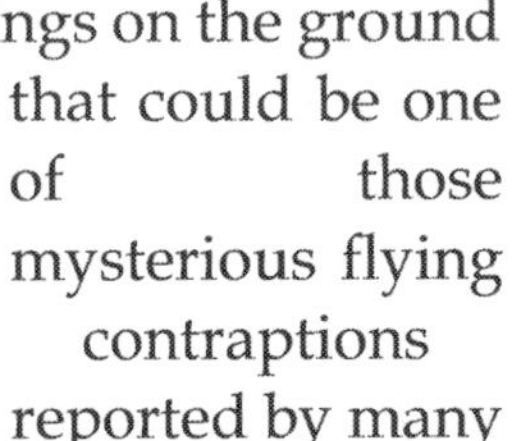

The Daily Times July 17, 1947

79 Yankton Press & Dakotan July 15, 1947

80 Denton record Chronicle July 16,1947

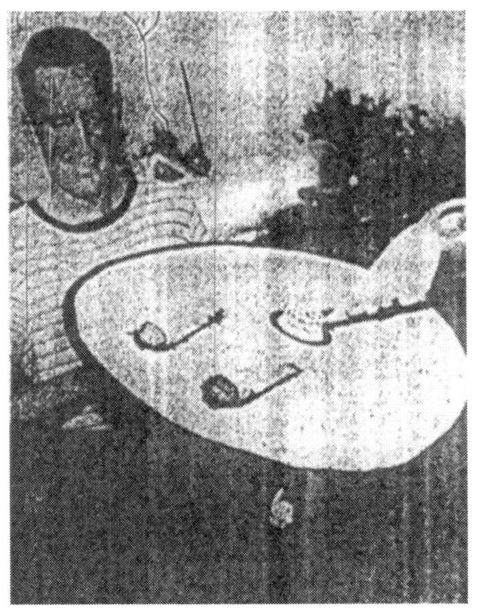

The Chattanooga Times July 18, 1947

Probably, it was a circular inspection opening top from a transport airplane that was jarred loose as it was flying in that vicinity[81].

Finding a disc was also an excellent way to promote an event. On July 17, a flying instructor at Chattanooga, Tennessee, claimed he "discovered and captured" a disc-shaped object at the local airport. Reporters commented that it could have something to do with the air show at the same place just a few days later[82].

The Chehalis Advocate July 17, 1947

A similar gag happened one or two days before at Chehalis, Washington. Chehalis Junior Chamber of Commerce members thought to exploit the saucer saga to promote their Lewis County Air Festival set for the following days. They created a large aluminum disc bearing appropriate advertising and placed it on a hillside to be "found" by two festival queen candidates[83].

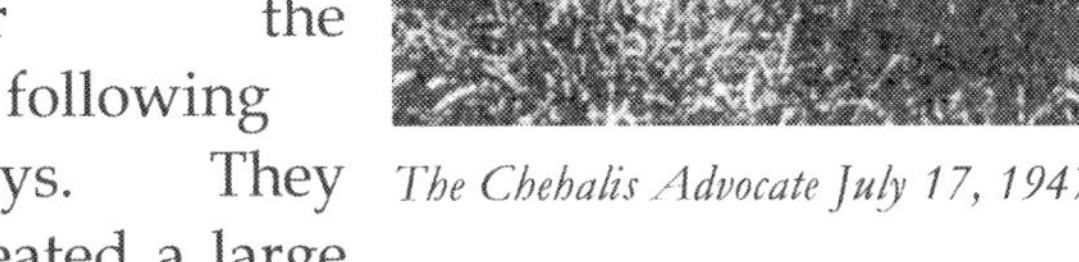

Hawk Eye Gazette July, 23 1947

---

81 The Daily Times July 17,1947

82 The Chattanooga Times July 18,1947

83 The Chehalis Advocate, The Centralia Daily Chronicle July 17,1947

Foto FBI del disco trovato a Saybrook

A lady named Harriett Dunham found a silver-colored contraption lying upside down in her front yard in Burlington, Iowa. At first, she thought it could be a bomb. It was rigged up with a radio tube, a can, and a condenser wired and soldered together in what looked like a 10-inch cake tin[84].

An unidentified lady from Saybrook, Illinois, reported to the Springfield FBI office the finding of a disc in her front yard in the early morning of July 26. An FBI agent went to the spot and wrote that the stability of the lady was questionable. He got the disc, and it was evident it was the work of some of the juveniles in the area. The object was an old wooden platter, which had assembled on it a silver plate, a spark plug, a timer, and some old brass tubing. The disc was on hold at the Springfield FBI office and was to be retained pending receipt of Bureau advice relative to its destruction[85].

'Disk' Found in Green Lake District Just Kirkland Stunt

MRS. FRANK OSTRANDER and "FLYING DISK"
This disk didn't fly; it was just for publicity

Seattle Daily Times July 8, 1947

PUBLICITY STUNTS

The American advertising industry quickly leveraged flying saucers to promote any products or services[86], mostly locally. Saucer-shaped paper plates dropped by airplanes were a favorite stunt to advertise events or to offer discounts.

---

84 Hawk Eye Gazette July 23, 1947

85 FBI Office Memorandum from SAC Springfield, dated August 20, 1947.

86 Verga, M. (2016) – "Come ti vendo il disco. 1947: i dischi volanti nella pubblicità". Cielo Insolito #2, 10-27

Star Tribune July 9, 1947

One of the first ones to be found was a bit different, though: it was a piece of sheet aluminum on which a small paper poster was pasted[87].

The poster advertised a local Summer Festival, and the promoting committee claimed it was attempting to capitalize on the curiosity aroused by the flying disk mystery to obtain cheap publicity.

More than 100 of these 14-inch-long ovals were left in strategic places all over Seattle. Likely on July 8, a man found a paper plate advertising Army recruiting without seeing it fluttering to the ground. The officers at the Minnesota-Dakota recruiting district said they knew nothing about that thing[88].

Just Like a Pie Plate

Flying Saucers Bombard City; Alert Air Raid Warden Recovers One

The Winona Republican Herald July 11, 1947

On July 10, a Minnesota newspaper ironically reported[89] a similar event involving the fall of several tens of paper plates that appeared to read:

> *Join the Civil Air Patrol. Army recruiting station, post office, Winona, Minn.*

Later in August, a few newspapers announced local drops of paper plates from civilian aircraft promoting Army recruiting or similar information[90].

---

87 Seattle Daily Times July 8,1947

88 Star Tribune July 9,1947

89 The Winona Republican Herald July 11,1947

90 The Ligonier Echo August 29, 1947

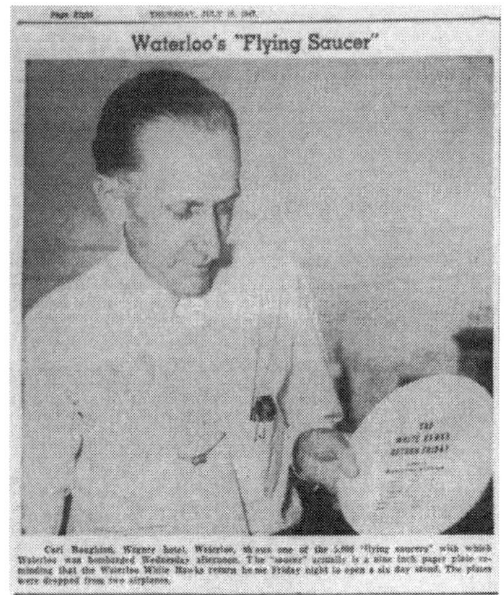

Waterloo Daily Courier July 10, 1947

Waterloo, Iowa, was bombarded[91] by about 5,000 9-inch paper "flying saucers" on the afternoon of July 9. Two airplanes dropped them to remind people of a local sports event.

A Florida newspaper[92] published the photo of a group of ladies throwing paper plates beside a parked plane.

On July 9, five planes dropped hundreds of those white and silver plates bearing inscriptions urging local voters to "Register and Vote Yes" in a referendum to be held on August 5 on the annexation of Tampa suburbs. Some residents called the newspaper to report sighting the famed flying discs.

The Tampa Tribune July 10, 1947

Even in Honolulu, Hawaii, large paper plates fell from the sky, this time to advertise local records.

One man said a disc ruined several valuable orchids, while hundreds of others were upset and called newspaper and radio offices[93].

91 Waterloo Daily Courier July 10,1947

92 The Tampa Tribune July 10,1947

93 Honolulu Star Bulletin July 12,1947

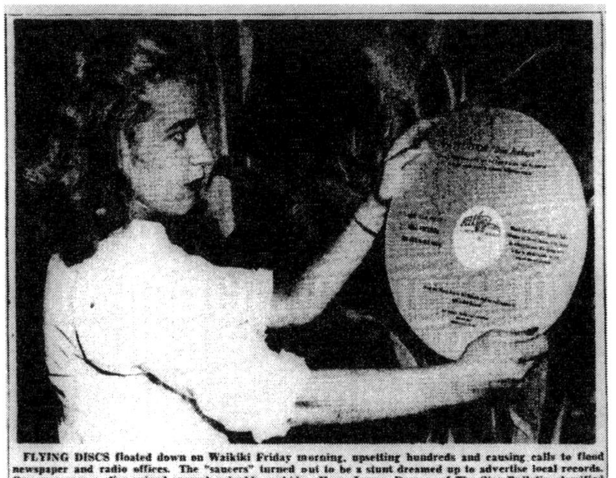

FLYING DISCS floated down on Waikiki Friday morning, upsetting hundreds and causing calls to flood newspaper and radio offices. The "saucers" turned out to be a stunt dreamed up to advertise local records. One man says a disc ruined several valuable orchids. Here, Jeanne Darrow of The Star-Bulletin classified advertising department, looks one over.—Star-Bulletin photo.

Honolulu Star Bulletin July 12, 1947

On July 16, 200 paper plates were scattered from a low-flying airplane over Falls Church, Virginia. They brought announcements of the town's September fiesta to raise funds for a public park. The photograph's caption introducing the news reads, "No cause for alarm."[94]

Around noon on July 19, about 3,000 12-inch cardboard disks were released over Casper, Wyoming. It was a massive advertising stunt promoted by a local car dealer. Those who retrieved the saucers read an invitation to ride in one of the new Frazier Manhattans cars[95].

Washington Post July 17, 1947

Casper Star Tribune July 20, 1947

Such stunts were used throughout October, although less frequently. Some local newspapers offered some funny photographs of what happened in those episodes.

---

94 Washington Post July 17,1947

95 Casper Star Tribune July 20, 1947

Estherville Daily News August 8, 1947

In early August, a caption titled "Typical scene on flying saucer day" introduced a photo with many adults and youngsters trying to snare one of the 300 disks released over Estherville, Iowa, from airplanes: the Junior Chamber of Commerce sponsored the event[96].

A local festival was promoted in Marshfield, Wisconsin, by the launch of hundreds of paper "flying saucers" each noon for three days. The discs allowed the lucky people finding them to redeem from 50 cents to $5 in merchandise.

A newspaper photo[97] depicted two employees showing some of those saucers to be scattered over the city. Several citizens of Allentown, Pennsylvania, found the paper plate dropped by a couple of planes on the streets a few days later. The plates had a text that read,

> *"This is not a flying saucer. But it is a reminder that this is Red Feather week. Have you made your pledge?"*[98]

The Marshfield News Herald October 15, 1947

---

96 Estherville Daily News August 8, 1947

97 The Marshfield News Herald October 15, 1947

98 The Allentown Morning Call October 19, 1947

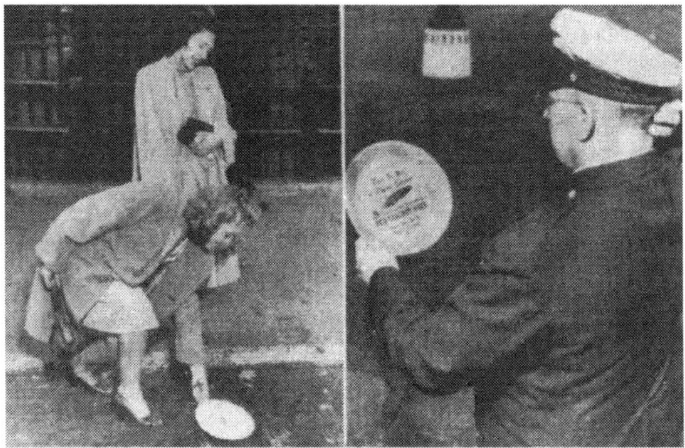

The Allentown Morning Call October 19, 1947

Scores of other paper plates were not launched from an airplane but set off from the Sear Roebuck tower in Minneapolis, Minnesota. According to the caption of a newspaper picture[99], "hundreds" of pedestrians were scrambling for them, but a close examination of the photo doesn't show such a frenzy.

The Minneapolis Star October 23, 1947

---

99 The Minneapolis Star October 23, 1947

Day one of the Saucer era in the press

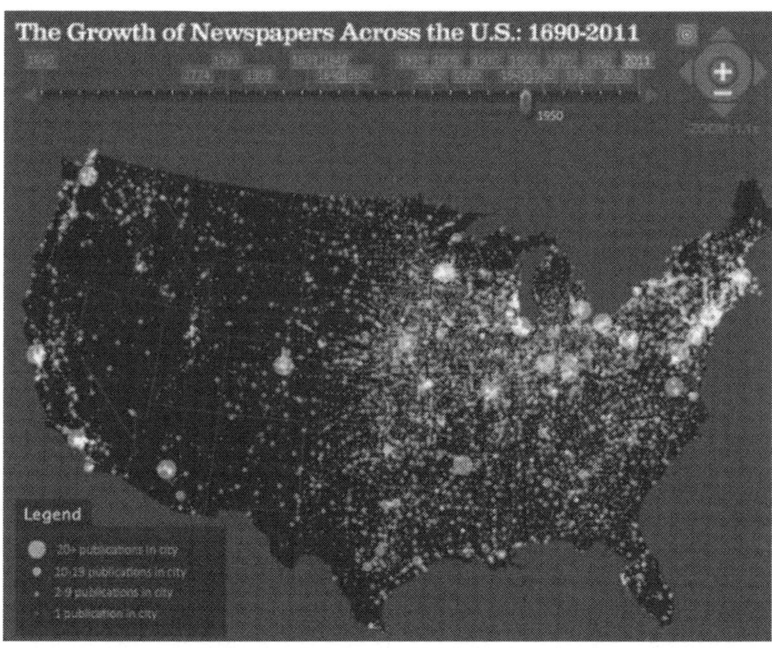

I didn't find precise figures about the number of newspapers published in the United States in 1947. Although the radio was an essential news medium, dailies were still in high numbers and likely the primary news source used by most people.

In 1950, three years later, the number of US newspapers was huge (yet nearly the same as today), 13,632, and distributed as in the map below[100]. Anyway, other sources provide very different figures, even eight times less, namely 1772[101].

The seminal Kenneth Arnold sighting, the starting point of the "flying saucer" mythology, occurred in the early afternoon of Tuesday, June 24, 1947. About 24 hours later, the very first article about the story was published by the small newspaper *East Oregonian* in Pendleton, Oregon. Its title was pretty neutral: *Impossible! Maybe, But Seein' Believin', Says Flyer*, without any specific clue about the reported sighting. Bill Bequette, the journalist who interviewed Arnold (when our man paid a visit to the newspaper office to tell what he had seen) and wrote the article, wired the story over the *Associated Press* network. That was the real trigger igniting the press and then the popular furor about the presence of mystery contraptions flying with impossible performances in the American skies.

Until very few years ago, the *East Oregonian* article was believed the very first one and the only one published on June 25.

---

100 http://www.aei.org/publication/interactive-map-of-u-s-newspapers-1690-2011/, last check on April 4, 2019.

101 https://www.journalism.org/numbers/number-of-u-s-daily-newspapers-5-year-increments/ on April 4, 2019.

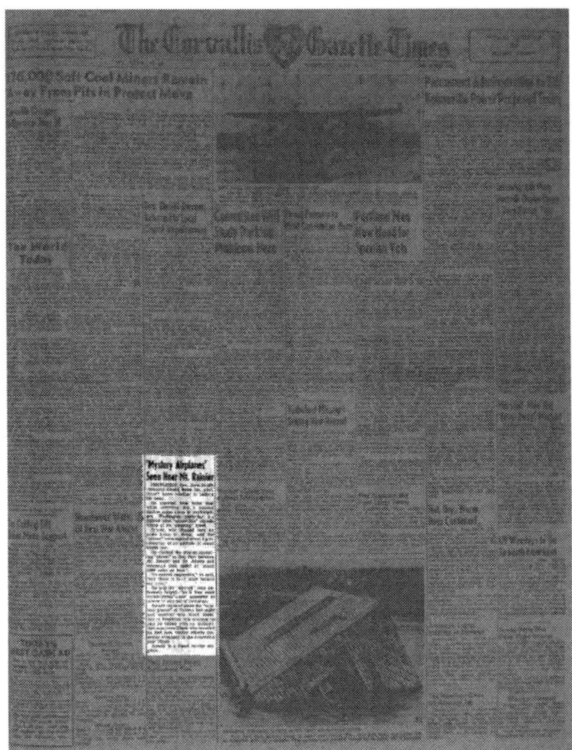
The Corvallis Gazette-Times

'Mystery Airplanes' Seen Near Mt. Rainier

The Corvallis Gazette 25 June 1947

Then another article was found, published by another Oregon newspaper[102], probably an afternoon or evening edition of it, just in time to be able to pick up and publish the *Associated Press* dispatch quickly. The *Corvallis Gazette* placed the article in the second half of the third column of its front page, using the title *'MYSTERY AIRPLANES' SEEN NEAR MT. RAINIER*. It openly suggested that something unusual was seen.

That same day, a few newspapers published Prof. Lyman Spitzer Jr.'s claims about space travel to Mars. His speech asserting that people from the red planet could have already been here had been quoted by other newspapers before that date, and others did later. Mentions about Mars and men from Mars were present in the newspapers in the previous June days and the earlier months.

On June 22, some newspapers[103] printed a nice advertisement about spaceship toys, letting kids dream about interplanetary travels.

On the morning of Thursday, June 26, hundreds of American newspapers printed the Arnold claims after the *Associated Press* dispatch. When writing this chapter (early 2019), 316 articles were on record, and 133 were printed on the front page. The 42% percentage sounds like a clear clue that the Arnold sighting was considered important news worth the front page.

---

102 The Corvallis Gazette June 25, 1947

103 The Philadelphia Enquirer, The Fresno Bee June 22, 1947

The Philadelphia Enquirer June 22, 1947

The overwhelming technological development and the continuous breakthroughs achieved by science helped people believe the strange story of a seemingly reliable witness, a pilot flying in his plane. Before them, journalists (who were exposed to the same dreams and wishful thinking) believed the story could be related to some weird new weapon.

After the shock of the atom bomb secrecy, people were ready to accept any further wonder and disbelieve any government denial of possible domestic secret weapons. Something extraordinary in the sky could be something like that or, worse, new Soviet planes. A small minority of people were ready to think of more exotic origins. Still, when newspapers introduced the concept of "Martian" in their articles, it was mainly related to the popular idea of something amazing and outperforming any known device or just for fun (although some articles and many letters from readers seemed to take it seriously). The same concept still survives today in popular culture.

FRONT PAGES

At first sight, the number of articles and the space devoted to the odd story of nine fast-flying "things" in the sky seen by an amateur pilot look unusual. After all, it was just the story of a man telling something strange he saw. Likely, he was the right witness in the right place at the right time.

Most articles were printed in the second half of the front pages, with few exceptions[104]. Although most were a single column with a few tens of lines (less frequently longer), many others were placed on two or (rarely) more columns, reprinting the original *Associated Press* dispatch at length. Two or

The Oregon Statesman

FOUNDED 1851

NINETY-SEVENTH YEAR — 14 PAGES — The Oregon Statesman, Salem, Ore., Thursday, June 26, 1947 — Price 5c — No. 78

Mystery Missiles Reported Over Cascades

Pilot Sees 'Disk-shaped Objects' Flying at 1200 Miles per Hour Above Western Washington Range

PENDLETON, Ore., June 25 -(AP)- Nine shiny objects flying at 1200 miles an hour over the Cascade range of western Washington—that's what Pilot Kenneth Arnold, Boise, Idaho, today reported he saw while on a routine flight over the mountains.

He stuck to his story tonight while experts said they had no explanation as to what the "objects" could be.

He said they were bright, saucer-like objects — he called them "aircraft"—flying at 10,000 feet altitude. A flash of reflected sunshine brought them to his attention and for a second he was stunned by their "incredible" speed, he told a reporter.

He rolled down the window of his plane, thinking it might have caused the reflection, but he still saw them with the window down, Arnold continued.

They flew with a peculiar dipping motion, "like a fish flipping in the sun," he said. "They were extremely shiny, and when they caught the sun right it nearly blinded me," he added.

He said they were about 25-30 miles away when first sighted flying south. He glanced at his instrument clock and timed them between Mt. Adams and Mt. Rainier, a distance of 47 miles, he said.

It took 1:42 minutes, Arnold reported, adding that after he landed, he got out a map and by triangulation figured the speed of the "objects" at 1200 miles an hour.

"I might have missed a second or two in my timing, but the speed still would be near 1,200 miles," he asserted.

In Portland, Ore., the state senior CAA inspector, Edward Leach, said he doubted "that anything would be traveling that fast."

Arnold also said a DC-4 was flying in the vicinity and he estimated the "objects" were about the same size as the four-engined passenger ships, although the "objects" did not have wings.

"One thing that struck me," he said, "was that they were flying so low. Ten thousand feet is very low for anything going at that speed."

He said they appeared to fly almost as if fastened together—if one dipped, the others did too.

Recently there have been several "mystery missile" reports in Oregon, one which fell on the Hill Military academy grounds in Portland later was attributed to a thaw blowing out an ice cap from a hollowed-out piece of metal. On another occasion a nurse in Vancouver, Wash., found a red-hot egg-shaped object. Geologists said it was not of meteorite composition. It never has been explained satisfactorily.

In Washington, the war department said it had no information on the Oregon sky mystery.

Arnold, a Boise businessman, who was searching for a missing plane, was flying a three-passenger, single-engined plane at the time.

Inquiries at Yakima last night brought only blank stares, he said. But he added he talked today with an unidentified man from Ukiah, south of here, who said he had seen similar objects over the mountains near Ukiah yesterday.

"It seems impossible," Arnold said, "but there it is."

The Oregon Statesman June 26, 1947

three-column articles were usually placed at the bottom of the front page.

A remarkable exception was *The Oregon Statesman*[105] (which extensively covered the growing flying saucer wave in the next two weeks). It published a five-column article with a large headline (*MYSTERY MISSILES REPORTED OVER CASCADES*) in the upper left part of the front page, also mentioning earlier retrievals of strange things falling from the sky.

104 The Montgomery Advertiser, The Baltimore Sun, Fort Myers News-Press, Milwaukee Sentinel, Altona Tribune June 26, 1947

105 The Oregon Statesman June 26, 1947

Bremerton Woman, 2 Midwest Men Say They Saw Disks

LABOR LAW MUST BE ENFORCED, SAYS TRUMAN, PLEDGING HIS AID

A. F. L., C. I. O. Reject General-Strike Pleas

SHOWERS

The Seattle Daily Times

NIGHT FINAL
LATE WORLD NEWS

SEATTLE, WASHINGTON, THURSDAY, JUNE 26, 1947. 3 SECTIONS, 36 PAGES PRICE FIVE CENTS

BOISE FLYER BACKED BY OBSERVERS

Senate Heeds Veto of Wool Bill; Passes New Measure

FAIR PLAY BY INDUSTRY, LABOR ASKED

262,000 Out As Shipyard Workers Join Coal Strikers

LABOR WILL FIGHT LAW IN COURTS

CURLEY LOSES STAY PLEA, ON WAY TO FEDERAL JAIL

The Seattle Daily Times June 26, 1947

A second exception was the night final edition of a Seattle newspaper[106], publishing a large headline on the top and through the whole width of the front page. A one-column-long article about sightings from other witnesses substantiating Arnold's story was placed on the top left of the front page. The interest in sighting those mysterious flying gadgets grew steadily throughout that Thursday.

Another final edition of an Oregon newspaper[107]published a giant headline on the front page, plus a couple of articles. Some newspapers from the North-West of the United States supplied extensive coverage immediately to that odd sighting. Maybe because those strange reports came from their courtyards, the chance the stories could be related to some sort of new super-weapon tested just in those regions led them to cover the news patriotically.

Disk Mystery Grows

Oregon Journal

2 MIDWEST MEN SUPPORT BOISE FLIER

Oregon Journal June 26, 1947

106 The Seattle Daily Times June 26, 1947

107 Oregon Journal June 26, 1947

The articles on the front pages remarked more frequently in their headlines the top flight performances of the objects in about one-third of them ("1,200 mph of speed", but many others used generic terms like "fast," "high-speed," "speedy") and the witness being a pilot, in more than 40% of the clippings.

The term "saucer" was used in about 14% of the titles printed on front pages: the idea of a "flying saucer" was amusing and likely attractive for the readers. Near half of all articles were placed on two or more columns, meaning they had more prominent, more visible titles and a consequent higher impact on the readers' attention and the assimilation of the news.

A sample of 133 articles published on June 26, 1947, on the front page of American newspapers.

1,200 mph	Saucer	Disc/Disk	Pilot	1-column	2+-column
32%	14%	3%	41%	50%	41%

A sample of 183 articles published on June 26, 1947, on the inside pages of American newspapers.

1,200 mph	Saucer	Disc/Disk	Pilot	1-column	2+-column
20%	8%	2%	29%	48%	38%

THE FLYING SAUCER IS BORN

The articles published on June 24 used headlines offering a variety of terms to describe the gadgets Arnold saw: planes, objects, missiles, pie pans, crafts, air mystery, projectiles, discs, and saucers, of course. According to the sample mentioned above, about 14% of the articles published on the front page included "saucers" or "saucer-shaped." Such a percentage is nearly half of the articles published in inner pages.

Although a minority, the idea of flying objects with a circular shape was immediately considered attractive and worth a position in the title by some headline writers. They misinterpreted the original *Associated Press* wire news, catching the saucer image out of the reported Arnold's claims.

The term was silly, familiar, and exotic at the same time. Rocket-like flying bodies would have been too obvious and relatively "normal" in those years of overwhelming technological achievements. They were a well-established image in popular culture, being the top spaceship model in most but all sci-fi comics. A shape like a disc or a sphere was aerodynamically acceptable and much more exotic, a strong clue of extraordinary science[108].

Arnold's words describing the objects he saw were unusual. They quickly became even stranger in the headlines, making the sighting (together with the out-of-this-world flight speed and a pilot as a witness) worth of interest and space in the newspapers. Without those ingredients and others (for example, the instantaneous appearance of "me-too" witnesses), the story would have died pretty soon in the pages of a local newspaper.

Alternative terms like "disk" and "disc" were rare that day. In the next two weeks, they were used by many newspapers once in a while, then they faded away pretty quickly, entirely replaced by "flying saucers," which had already become part of the popular culture of the time, in just a couple of weeks or less.

In the body of the articles, the original Arnold's description of the object shape was rarely printed[109]:

> *[...] They were half-moon-shaped, oval in front and convex in the rear.*

FLYING FASTER THAN ANYTHING

Besides the presence of a pilot witnessing an unusual phenomenon showing an unconventional shape, there was another key element: the reported terrific speed performances. The top speed of the jet airplanes of the time was below 600 mph, although rumors about attempts to break the sound barrier had been around for some time.

---

108 That may be why some spaceships depicted on pulp magazine covers from the 1920s and 1930s are so similar to later flying saucer stories and images.

109 The Press and Democrat June 26, 1947

Walter Winchell, a noted columnist of the *New York Daily Mirror*, wrote an article (reprinted by some other American dailies[110]) suggesting the flying saucers were a new military secret weapon, a flying wing developed by the Navy. He also added a fascinating story:

> *It is also alleged that in 1943 an American firm (in Chicago) pioneering in jet propulsion planes sent an experimental test ship through the so-called supersonic wall.*
> *In other words, in this test flight in 1943 the pet plane traveled with a pilot aboard faster than sound. Thus it supposedly went through the 'wall' where it was traveling in space ahead of itself. While I have not confirmed information on the above, I understand these facts are in existence and that the plane was not heard of again for more than three weeks when it was found crashed somewhere in lower Montana. The pilot was dead. He was 38. but his teeth and body were those of a man of 25. He got younger, not older.*

Twice the speed of the fastest planes around was the ultimate clue that the Arnold story was extraordinary. So much to be worth the privileged space on the front pages and to catch the attention of other would-be witnesses telling their own stories and then generating a snowball effect of news-generating sightings and sightings causing news.

Odd-shaped objects flying at low speed, seen in the distance by an ordinary man, probably would have resulted in no follow-up, especially if the case had happened in another country.

The 1,200 mph feature was included and emphasized in the headlines of about one-third of all articles published on the front page and about one-fifth of those placed on the inside pages. That out-of-this-world speed was likely a piece of catchy news. In many other headlines, there were more generic yet similar terms, like “speedy” or “fast,” while the 1,200 mph velocity was a constant in the text of all articles. In headlines, "mystery" or "mysterious" were frequently used to accentuate the feeling of strangeness. Still, they were frequently counterbalanced by mentioning the authorities' quick skepticism regarding the odd event. Other papers remarked in the titles that the story puzzled the authorities or the witness himself, suggesting something weird behind it.

---

110 The Minneapolis Star, Camden Courier Post July 10,1947; The Philadelphia Enquirer July 11,1947

PILOT

The press emphasized the fact that the story had been reported by a pilot (although an amateur one) while flying in the sky.

Pilot (or flyer or airman) was the keyword. The word from a businessman flying aboard his plane was pretty trustworthy. Fliers definitely had a better reputation for reporting things in the sky than anybody else. If Arnold had said something flying in the sky, something strange was actually up there. This is likely one of the reasons because 41% of the front page articles and 29% of those printed on the inside pages had the word "pilot" (or equivalent) in their headlines. One newspaper defined Arnold as a "ranger"[111] in the article headline, while many others introduced him as a "United States Forest Service employee." Some articles introduced Arnold as a "bug-eyed pilot[112]," while one at least printed a headline describing the man's real job: *SALESMAN REPORTS FLYING OBJECTS*[113].

MARS AS A RHETORICAL IMAGE OF EXTRAORDINARY

Men From Mars? Sky Whizzer Seen!

PENDLETON, Ore., June 26.—(AP)—A tale of nine mysterious objects—big as airplanes—whizzing over western Washington at 1200 miles an hour got skepticism today from the army and air experts.

The man who reported the objects, Kenneth Arnold, a flying Boise, Idaho, businessman, clung, however, to his story of the shiny, flat objects, each as big as a DC-4 passenger plane, racing over Washington's Cascade mountains with a peculiar weaving motion "like the tail of a kite".

MAY BE ROCKET.

An army spokesman in Washington, D. C., commented, "as far as we know, nothing flies that fast except a V-2 rocket, which travels at about 3500 miles an hour and that's too fast to be seen".

The spokesman added that the V-2 rockets would not resemble the objects reported by Arnold, and that no high-speed experimental tests were being made in the area where Arnold said the objects were.

LIKE PIE-PAN.

Arnold described the objects as "flat like a pie-pan," and so shiny that they reflected the sun like a mirror.

He said he was flying east at 2:59 p. m. two days ago toward Mt. Rainier when they appeared directly in front of him 25 to 30 miles away at 10,000 feet altitude.

By his plane's clock he timed them at 1:42 minutes for the 47 miles from Mt. Rainier to Mt. Adams, Arnold said, adding that he later figured by triangulation that their speed was 1200 miles an hour.

The San Antonio Light June 26, 1947

The attractive title *MEN OF MARS? BOIESAN SEES SPEED PLANES* [114] popped up on the bottom part of the front page of a newspaper but nothing else in the body of the article. Martians were not really considered the origin of the sighting. Yet, the reported flying contraptions were so weird in performances that they were as fantastic (and unlikely) as the popular idea of "men from Mars."

A Texan newspaper[115] had a similar headline on the bottom front page, and once again, there was nothing about Martians in the text.

---

111 The San Francisco Examiner June 26, 1947

112 The Amarillo Globe June 26, 1947

113 The Provo Daily Herald June 26, 1947

114 Twin Falls Times News June 26, 1947

115 The San Antonio Light June 26, 1947

The title of a one-column article in another newspaper[116] was *PILOT SEE PLANES FROM OTHER WORLD.*

A Canadian paper printed a headline about a popular sci-fi hero reminiscent of super-science from out of this world: *SHADES OF FLASH GORDON!*[117] It was likely related to the 1,200 mph speed outperforming anything from this world.

In the opening of the article about the Arnold story, a newspaper wrote [118]:

> *Nine saucer-shaped Martian planes reported seen in southwest Washington at 10,000 feet late Tuesday by a Boise, Idaho, airplane pilot, were "out of this world."*

MORE WITNESSES, THE SAGA BEGINS

Another *United Press* wire service news was printed in some newspapers' afternoon and evening editions: other people claimed unusual sightings similar to Arnold's.

For example, Byron Savage from Oklahoma City, Oklahoma, told about a flat, disc-like object flying at a terrific speed about the dusk of five or six weeks before[119]. Savage was introduced as a "businessman pilot,"[120] ed affermò:

> *I know that boy up there (Arnold) really saw them. I kept quite after that (his sighting) until I read about that man seeing nine of the same things I saw and I thought it only fair to back him up.*

A carpenter from Kansas City, Missouri, W.I. Davenport, reported a sighting of nine flying objects leaving a vapor trail that happened on June 25[121]. Mrs. Elma Shingler, a lady from Bremerton, Washington, claimed to have seen "platter-like" objects hurtling through the sky at tremendous speed on June 17 and 24[122].

---

116 La Grande Evening Observer June 26, 1947

117 The Vancouver Sun (Canada) June 26, 1947

118 The Minneapolis Star June 26, 1947

119 The Lawton Constitution, Morning Olympian, Bellingham Herald June 26, 1947

120 The Miami News-Record, The Denver Post June 26, 1947

121 Spokane Daily Chronicle, Oregon Journal, Corvallis Gazette Times June 26, 1947

122 The Seattle Daily Times June 26, 1947

The story broke the ice, and more and more people began remembering something strange they believed to have seen in the sky and felt fully authorized to tell their story, finally, and become part of the news. The additional sightings reported by the press on June 26 came from *Associated Press* news.

Printed in Great Britain
by Amazon

2ffe8798-f0fb-4ab7-82a5-e0cd9fba1c36R01